THE FORTY DAYS
FOLLOWING THE RESURRECTION

John Bligh

THE FORTY DAYS
Following the Resurrection

ST PAULS

ST PAULS Publishing
187 Battersea Bridge Road, London SW11 3AS, UK
www.stpauls.ie

Copyright © ST PAULS 2007

ISBN 978 85 439 7257 2

Set by TuKan DTP, Stubbington, Hampshire, UK
Printed in Malta by Progress Press Company Limited

ST PAULS is an activity of the priests and brothers
of the Society of St Paul who proclaim the Gospel
through the media of social communication

CONTENTS

Foreword   7

The Resurrection Narrative of the Fourth Gospel   10
   Synoptic Anticipations of these Johannine Stories   19

The Synoptic Tradition   25
   Retrojected Narratives and Discourses   27

The Resurrection Narrative of M1   40
   Reconstruction: from the Empty Tomb
      to Pentecost   40
   Galilean Anticipations of the Resurrection
      Narrative of M1   46
   The Expectations of the Disciples after Pentecost   57
      Geographical Note   59

M2's Revision of the Work of M1   60
   The Resurrection Narrative of M2:
      from the Empty Tomb to the Ascension 65

M3's Revision of the Work of M2   69
   The Expectations of M3   71
   The Resurrection Narrative of M3: from the
      Empty Tomb to the Mountain in Galilee 73
   M3's Resurrection Narrative and his
      Infancy Narrative   78

The Resurrection Narrative of M4 (canonical Matthew):
   from the Empty Tomb to the Mountain in Galilee 81

The Resurrection Narrative of Mark:
   the Empty Tomb, and the Longer Ending   83

The Resurrection Narrative of Luke:
   from the Empty Tomb to the Ascension   86

The Resurrection Narrative of the Acts of the Apostles:
   from the Resurrection to Pentecost   91

Afterword   99

Foreword

According to Luke 24:46-48, the eleven apostles were sent forth to testify to the fulfilment of the Scriptures in the Death and Resurrection of Jesus the Messiah. Their witness to his Passion and Death is preserved in the Passion Narratives of the four Gospels, which agree with one another on all substantial points, though they rarely advert to the fulfilment of the Scriptures. But the Resurrection Narratives are different: each of the four evangelists goes his own way. According to St Matthew, Jesus appeared to Mary Magdalene and other women near the tomb outside Jerusalem, then once to the disciples a few days later on a mountain in Galilee. From St Luke's Gospel it appears that Jesus appeared only on Easter Sunday – to Peter, to the two travellers to Emmaus, and in the late evening to the disciples altogether, this last appearance ending with his Ascension that very evening. According to St John, he appeared to Mary Magdalene on Easter morning, to the disciples without Thomas on Easter evening, to the disciples with Thomas eight days later, and to Peter and six others beside the Sea of Galilee some time later; in this Gospel the Appearances the evangelist has chosen to relate are extended over about twelve to fifteen days. But according to the Acts of the Apostles, Jesus appeared to his disciples "during forty days, speaking of the kingdom of God." According to Paul, Jesus also appeared on one occasion to more than five hundred brethren at one time (1 Cor 15:6). The discrepancy between the Infancy Narratives of Matthew and Luke, though equally surprising, is much less significant, since the stories of the Birth and Childhood of Jesus are not part of the official apostolic witness, as is the Resurrection (see Lk 24:45-48; Acts 1:22). If we had only Matthew, or only Luke, we should understand that after his Resurrection Jesus appeared to his eleven remaining disciples on only one occasion, on a mountain in Galilee according to Matthew, behind closed doors in Jerusalem according to Luke.

The lack of agreement among the chief witnesses to the Resurrection is liable to undermine a student's confidence in the reliability of the evangelists and of the Church that endorses them – particularly if the student accepts the Two-Source Theory, according to which the Gospel of St Mark is the first Gospel that was ever written. According to this theory, which the present writer does not accept, St Matthew and St Luke used Mark as their major source,[1] but as Mark ends abruptly without narrating any appearance of the Risen Jesus, they were forced to invent narratives of Resurrection Appearances; they did so independently of each other and inevitably produced results that cannot be harmonised. The Two-Source Theory, if accepted, leads logically to the conclusion that the narratives of Jesus' post-Resurrection Appearances are pious fictions, unreliable as history, and therefore a weak foundation for any apologetic or theological argument.

The purpose of this booklet is to re-examine the four Resurrection Narratives in the light of a different theory (see pp. 25-26), which will make it possible to find out how such wide divergences occurred, and to reconstruct the earliest account of what happened in the forty days. The booklet is short, but the research that lies behind it is multi-voluminous, as my literary executors will discover.

In the writing of a monograph such as this, the order of exposition rarely coincides with the order of discovery. I propose to begin my exposition with the Fourth Gospel, which claims, formally and credibly, to offer a participant's report of the events narrated (Jn 19:35; 21:24). The text as we have it was probably put together late in the first century, and one part of it (21:20-23) was certainly composed at that time, but other parts were written much earlier and were almost certainly known to writers of the Synoptic tradition, as will be seen. Indeed, at an early stage, they were parts of the Synoptic tradition. The Fourth Gospel is much more closely akin to the Synoptic Gospels than is commonly recognised.

The upshot of this investigation will be to vindicate the credibility of the Resurrection Narratives and therefore the reasonableness of faith in the Resurrection of Christ.

The Resurrection Narrative of the Fourth Gospel

The Resurrection Narrative of the Fourth Gospel consists of the following items:

20:1-2   Mary Magdalene finds the tomb empty and reports to Simon Peter and the beloved disciple.

20:3-10   They run to investigate and come away believing in the Resurrection.

20:11-18   Jesus appears to Mary Magdalene at the tomb and sends her to his disciples with the message, "I am ascending to my Father and your Father, my God and your God."

20:19-23   Jesus appears to ten disciples in the absence of Thomas, puts new Spirit into them, and gives them power to forgive sins.

20:24-28   Jesus appears to the ten with Thomas. He overcomes the disbelief of Thomas, who worships him.

20:30-31   Conclusion to the Gospel.

21:1-14   Jesus appears to Peter and six others at the Sea of Galilee. He makes Peter shepherd of the whole flock.

21:15-23   Jesus speaks of the future of Peter but not of the Beloved Disciple. [Transfiguration-Ascension]

21:24-25   Second Conclusion to the Gospel.

It is frequently conjectured that the fourth evangelist planned his Gospel to conclude with a short Resurrection Narrative ending in Jerusalem, without any return to Galilee, and that he added the Appearance at the Sea of Galilee as an afterthought. This is highly plausible, because Jn 20:30-31 would make a splendid conclusion to the book. Nevertheless, the conjecture is probably incorrect. The fourth evangelist planned his whole Gospel as a reverse parallelism, and the Appearance at the Sea of Galilee is a necessary part of this structure, as was shown in *Gospel Challenges*, pp. 237-38. Jn 21:1-23 at the end matches Jn 1:35-46 at the beginning.[2] In the earlier of these two texts Jesus gathers his flock; in the later he hands over the flock to Peter as shepherd. In 1:39 he entertains his first two disciples; in 21:9 he prepares a meal for the seven; in 1:39 he invites two disciples to "come and see" where he is staying, and in 21:19, he says, "Follow me!" The miraculous catch in the later passage reminds the Beloved Disciple of the earlier miraculous catch (Lk 5:47). Jesus reveals who he is by what he does, as he tells doubters in Jn 10:25.

By "the fourth evangelist" is here meant the editor who constructed the canonical Gospel according to John about AD 90 out of texts written by an eyewitness at various times in the preceding decades. (This editor is responsible for some awkward transitions, e.g. from Jn 20:10 to 20:11.)

It was also shown in *Gospel Challenges* that between 21:23 and 21:24 something is missing, namely, an item to match 1:6-34 at the beginning. As the Prologue is a commentary on the Transfiguration narrative and Jn 6:62 points forward to an Ascension narrative, it is extremely likely that at one stage of composition the fourth evangelist meant to include a Transfiguration-Ascension narrative (like the one in the Apocalypse of Peter) as the closing scene of his Gospel.

A conclusion not drawn in *Gospel Challenges* is that 21:24, in which the writer asserts that he was present at the events narrated, means that he claimed to be an eye-witness, not only of the death and burial of Jesus, but also of his Resurrection Appearances, including his Transfiguration and Ascension.

> He who has seen has borne witness, and his witness is true, and he knows that he speaks the truth, that you too may believe (19:35).
>
> This is the disciple who bears witness about these things and wrote these things (*grapsas tauta*): [*Signature*]. And we know that his witness is true: [*Signatures of presbyters*] (21:24).

These are extremely important declarations. The evangelist declares that he has put together first-hand, eyewitness reports of the central events of the Gospel story, and his declaration was endorsed, it seems, by the signatures of others, who knew that his testimony was reliable.

The closing verse (21:25) is also worthy of close attention. What it states is not a wild exaggeration, since Jesus is the Word described in Jn 1:1, without whom nothing was made or done. But further, taken together with the earlier conclusion (20:

30-31), it casts light on the evangelist's conception of a "Gospel". His book does not pretend to be a complete account (*diegesis*) of the Life, Death and Resurrection of Jesus; it is a selection of certain events drawn together to persuade readers that Jesus is the Christ the Son of God, so that believing they may have life in his name. The evangelist could narrate many other such events, but these are enough and more than enough to support faith.

Now some comments on various part of this Resurrection Narrative.

Peter and John investigate the Tomb

There is here the same careful exposition of who did what first as there was in Jn 1:35-51. This is an attempt, no doubt, to resolve disputes among over-eager supporters of one apostle against another, but at the same time, unintentionally and indirectly, it is evidence that the writer of this story was a participant in the events narrated.

Jesus' Appearance to Mary Magdalene

There is a touch of humour here (as in the Emmaus story, Lk 24:18). Mary takes Jesus for the cemetery-keeper and says: "Tell me where he has been moved to, and I'll take him away." Then, as Mary recognises him, Jesus replies, "Oh no you won't – I haven't yet ascended to my Father. Go and tell my brothers, that I am going up to my Father and your Father, to my God and your God." The words formally translated, "Do not touch me!" are Jesus' response to Mary's "I will take him away" (presumably to where the male disciples are hiding). The message that Jesus sends appears to be an explanation of why he will not rejoin his disciples till evening (20:19): he must first ascend to his Father, implying that he has not yet done so. There was disagreement among the earliest disciples as to when Jesus ascended to his Father: directly from the Cross (Lk 23:43), or on the day of his Resurrection (as here), or at the end of the Forty Days. (Mt 27:53 appears to have been composed by someone who took the first view, and "corrected" by someone who took the second.)

Jesus' Appearance to his Disciples in Jerusalem

The disciples are in hiding behind closed doors "for fear of the Jews," when Jesus appears in the midst of them. He breathes his own Spirit into them to release them from fear. The scene is symbolic of the release of sinners from fear of God's punishment when their sins are forgiven. (It may also be symbolic of Jesus' appearance in Limbo to release the souls of the just, as mentioned in the Creeds.) As the Father has sent him with power, so he empowers his disciples to go forth and forgive sinners.[3]

In this scene Jesus converts his timid disciples into courageous preachers of the gospel, partly by a sacramental insufflation, but also by means of his words: "You are the light of the world," "You are the salt of the earth" – believe it, and you will find it is true! These powerful words, preserved in the Sermon on the Mount, really belong to the post-Resurrection period.[4]

The Appearance to Thomas

A week later, by which time they may have moved to Galilee, the disciples are again behind closed doors, but there is no more mention of fear of the Jews. Jesus appears again, convinces Thomas, and pronounces one more beatitude: "Blessed are those who have not seen and have believed" (20:29) – a word of reproach to Thomas but of comfort to others, leading perfectly into the splendid, resounding conclusion in 20:30-31.

There is a close resemblance between this scene near the end of the Gospel and Jesus' encounter with Nathanael near the beginning (Jn 1:45-51). The promise made by Jesus in 1:51 had its fulfilment in the Transfiguration-Ascension narrative when it was part of the conclusion of this Gospel.

This Appearance also includes a preliminary fulfilment of the prophetic words, "They will look on him who was pierced" (Zech 12:10; Jn 19:36), which will have a further fulfilment at the Parousia (Apoc 1:7).

The Transfiguration Narrative

Matthew, Mark and Luke all record Peter's inappropriate response to the glorious vision of Jesus, Moses and Elijah: "Lord, it is good for us to be here; let us make three tabernacles (*skenas*), one for you, one for Moses, and one for Elijah." St Mark regards this as nonsense, since he comments, "For he did not know how to respond." St Matthew gives no comment or explanation, and St Luke gives the laughable explanation that the three disciples fell asleep, and Peter waking up suddenly, responded with random words. But why do they record his foolish words if they lead to nothing? Does St Luke mean that the three apostles were so bored with the conversation between Jesus, Moses and Elijah that they fell asleep? More probably he means that while Jesus prayed, the three fell asleep, just as they did in Gethsemane, then Moses and Elijah appeared, and when Peter suddenly woke up, he saw the three figures in glory. In that case, Jesus must have told him later what he had been discussing with Moses and Elijah. The narration is quite confused.

Probably all three evangelists, Matthew, Mark and Luke, have given their readers a garbled account of what the fourth evangelist originally wrote. In the original narrative, Jesus took with him Peter "and two others" (unnamed as in Jn 21:2), and one of them was the Beloved Disciple (implied in Jn 21:24).[5] His reason for including Peter's inappropriate comment was either: (1) to make Peter look foolish – which seems unlikely, or (2) to draw a contrast between the serious conversation of Jesus with Moses and Elijah and the trivial remark of Peter, or (3) to show that even at this stage Peter still thinks it a great honour for Jesus to associate with such historic figures as Moses and Elijah. Moses – Elijah – Jesus! What a glorious trinity! If this third conjecture is correct, Peter's mistake evokes an indignant protest from God the Father in the name of the heavenly Trinity: "This is not another prophet; this is my beloved Son!

Forget them; hear him!" (4) A further possibility is that the Voice from heaven originally replied, with less indignation: "Here is the tabernacle of God with men (in the person of Jesus), and he will dwell with them; they shall be his people, and he their 'God with them' (Emmanuel); this is my beloved Son, in whom I am well pleased; hear him!" (Apoc 21:3; Mt 17:5.)

At all events, the author of the text seems to have intended to draw contrasts between what Moses, Elijah and Jesus say, what Peter says, and what the Voice from heaven says.

As was noted above, the Prologue of the Fourth Gospel is a commentary on the Transfiguration, in which the disciples "saw his glory" (Lk 9:32; Jn 1:14), and Peter's remark about tabernacles recalls the earlier part of Jn 1:14, "The Word became flesh and tabernacled (*eskenosen*) among us."

Another question arising from the garbled narrative is: What is the point of the descent of the cloud as Peter wakes up and the Voice is heard from heaven repeating the words heard by John the Baptist at the Baptism of Jesus? A possible answer is that this was the moment when the three disciples were baptised with the Spirit (cf. 1 Cor 10:2). If so, the Baptist's promise of Spirit-baptism (Jn 1:33) did not remain unfulfilled at the end of this Gospel.

The Appearance at Lake Tiberias (the Sea of Galilee)

Peter goes fishing with Thomas, Nathanael, James and John, and two unnamed others, one of whom is the Beloved Disciple (21:20). Jesus gives them a miraculous catch and the Beloved Disciple, recognising Jesus by what he does, exclaims, "It is the Lord!" By a fireside in the early morning, Peter make a threefold declaration of love, cancelling out his three denials, and Jesus makes him shepherd of the whole flock.

Jesus speaks of the future of Peter but not of the Beloved Disciple

This is the paragraph written later in the apostolic era. Christians are still expecting the imminent return of Jesus as Judge, and some think he will return before the Beloved Disciple tastes death. To discourage such expectations, and to ensure that his death will not undermine anyone's faith, the evangelist inserts 21:20-23. As in the other gospels, the Risen Jesus does not answer questions put to him by his disciples. He obscurely prophesies the death of Peter, but refuses to prophesy the future of the Beloved Disciple: "If I want him to remain till I come, what is that to you? You follow me!"

The Final Supper and the Prayer of the Departing Revealer

If the fourth evangelist intended at one stage to end with the Ascension, as Jn 6:62 suggests, no doubt it was preceded by a final Supper (cf. Acts 10:41), which would be the perfect setting for Jesus' prayer in Jn 17, "the Prayer of the Departing Revealer", as Bultmann called it:

I have glorified you upon earth, completing the work that you gave me to do; and now do you, Father, glorify me in your presence with the glory I had with you when the world was not. (Jn 17:4-5)

SYNOPTIC ANTICIPATIONS OF THESE JOHANNINE STORIES

Though it is undoubtedly correct to assign a late date to the "publication" (in Greek *ekdosis*, the "giving out") of the Fourth Gospel, it does not follow that the Resurrection stories built into it are of late date. Some are probably of very early date. The Fourth Gospel does not represent a separate tradition that has only slight links with the Synoptic tradition, as is commonly said. There is good evidence that some of the stories preserved in the Fourth Gospel belonged to the Synoptic tradition at an early stage, were for various reasons (to be explored) dropped by later evangelists, and finally salvaged by the fourth evangelist.

In all four Gospels there are events in the public ministry that point forward to events on Calvary and in the Resurrection Narratives. These earlier events can be conveniently referred to as "Anticipations". Several examples of such Anticipations preserved in the Synoptic gospels point forward to the Resurrection stories of the Fourth Gospel. Consider the following.

A Search for Jesus, Mk 1:35-38

> And early, while it saw still night, rising up he went out to a desert place and there was praying. Peter and those with him tracked him down; they found him and said to him, "Everyone is searching for you." He said to them: "Let us go elsewhere to the nearby villages [*komopoleis*] that I may preach there too, for it was for this that I came forth."

This little story is pointless except as pointing forward to Jn 20:1-20, where Jesus rises up early while it is still night, and Mary Magdalene, Peter and the Beloved Disciple search for him. When eventually he meets Mary Magdalene, he refuses to go with her to where she wants, because this time he must go back to the presence for the Father from which he came forth – a hint of the divine origin of Jesus.[6]

Another possibility is that this incident originally pointed forward to a (lost) Appearance to Peter just before the Journey to Emmaus (Lk 24:13), a place that could well be described as a *komopolis*.

Cure of a Paralytic; Forgiveness of Sins, Mk 2:1-11; Mt 9:1-8

> Mark 2:1 – And when he came into Capharnaum again a few days later, people heard that he was at home, and many came together, so that it was no longer possible to get to the door, and he was speaking the Word to them.

> And four people carrying a paralytic came to him, and not being able to bring him to Jesus because of the crowd, they removed the roof where he was, and having cleared it away, they let down the stretcher on which the paralytic was lying. Jesus, seeing their faith, said to the paralytic, "Child, your sins are forgiven" [Jesus cures him].
>
> Matthew 9:8 – And the crowds who saw this were struck with fear and gave glory to God who had given such power to men.

This much more elaborate story points forward to the post-Resurrection scene in the Fourth Gospel where the disciples are behind closed doors through fear of the Jews, and Jesus appears mysteriously in their midst (entering through the roof?), forgives them for deserting him during his Passion, and imparts to them the power to forgive others (Jn 20:23). Canonical Matthew, probably unaware of this link (as of the last), omitted the details about the removal of the roof, thinking them irrelevant.

The Compassion of Jesus, Mt 10:36-37

> Seeing the crowds, he had pity on them, because they were harried and torn like sheep without a shepherd. Then he said to his disciples, "The harvest is great, the workers few; pray then the Lord of the harvest that he send workers into his harvest."

This saying points forward to the Appearance of Jesus to the Ten, when he says to them, "As the Father sent me, so I send you" (20:21). It did not originally point forward to the Sending of the Twelve that immediately follows in Matthew, when no one has had time to pray for harvesters. (Matthew has similarly placed the Transfiguration much too soon after Mt 16:28).

The Parable of the Sulky Children, Mt 11:16-19

> To what shall I liken this generation? They are like children sitting in the market-place who cry to one another, "We have piped to you and you have not danced; we have mourned and you would not beat your breasts."

This has immediate reference to the Galileans who responded neither to John the Baptist nor to Jesus, but it also fits Thomas, who refused to participate in the joy of the other disciples who had seen Jesus and were delighted to know that he was risen. For a whole week, doubting Thomas maintained an obstinate sulk. (He was in much the same mood in Jn 11:16, when he thought Jesus was walking to his death.)

The Parable of the Faithful Servant, Mt 25:45-47

> Who then is the faithful and prudent servant whom the Lord placed over all his servants to give them food at the right time? Blessed is that servant whom the Lord at his coming

> finds so doing. I tell you, he will place him in charge of all his property.

The direct reference may be to the Second Coming of Jesus at the end of time, but the parable also has a preliminary fulfilment in the Appearance at Lake Tiberias, when Peter has laboured all night to get his companions something to eat, and after breakfast Jesus places him in charge of his whole flock, sheep as well as lambs.

[The miraculous catch in Jn 21:4-7 points back to Lk 5:1-10, rather than vice versa.]

Peter's Denials, Mk 14:54

> Peter followed him at a distance right into the courtyard of the High Priest, and was sitting with the servants warming himself at the fire. [Lk 22:55 also mentions the fire.]

The point of this little detail (which Matthew omits) is that Peter denies Jesus in the early hours of the morning beside a fire, as later he makes his threefold profession of love in the early hours of the morning beside a fire in Galilee.

The Baptist's Question, Mt 11:2-3

> John, having heard in prison what Jesus was doing, sent his disciples to ask, "Are you the One who was to Come, or shall we await another?"

John is really concerned about what Jesus is not doing: he is not administering the Spirit-baptism announced by John. His question receives its definitive answer in the Transfiguration narrative, when the Voice from heaven repeats the revelation given to him at the Baptism: "This is my beloved Son in whom I am well pleased; hear him!" The link is even stronger if the disciples present at the Transfiguration receive in the cloud the Spirit-Baptism prophesied by John.

The Synoptic Tradition

Gospel Challenges presented an alternative theory of the prehistory of canonical Matthew, which may be summed up as follows. Matthew is not a conflation of Mark and the hypothetical Q. Both canonical Matthew and Mark are dependent upon an early draft of Matthew (M1) that was written within a decade of Pentecost; the second edition (M2) was written while Paul and Barnabas were evangelising the Gentiles of Asia Minor, by a writer who did not approve of what they were doing; the third (M3) was written after the Council of Jerusalem in AD 49/50 had approved the missionary policy and work of Paul; and the fourth (M4 or canonical Matthew) is a lightly revised version of M3, designed to make the text more suitable for liturgical use, e.g. by omitting seemingly irrelevant details, by making the disciples show more reverence for Jesus, and by removing any possible suggestion that his power was limited. On the basis of this alternative theory, which allows that "many" before Luke had written up the gospel story (Lk 1:1), it is possible to reconstruct the succession of events during the forty days and to explain why the canonical evangelists chose to shorten it, reproducing what they did and no more than they did. Unlike the Two-Source theory, this theory of Four Stages in the Composition of Matthew does not lead to scepticism about the reliability of the Resurrection Narratives.

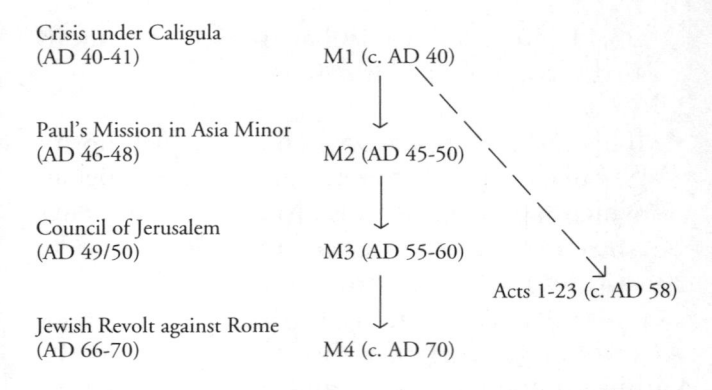

Crisis under Caligula (AD 40-41)	M1 (c. AD 40)	
Paul's Mission in Asia Minor (AD 46-48)	↓ M2 (AD 45-50)	
Council of Jerusalem (AD 49/50)	↓ M3 (AD 55-60)	
		Acts 1-23 (c. AD 58)
Jewish Revolt against Rome (AD 66-70)	↓ M4 (c. AD 70)	

The earliest evangelist (M1) attempted to preserve the chronological sequence of events as far as he could. Revisers upset his order and introduced discourses that do not fit into their immediate context because they are really addressed to readers of a later generation. Attempts to preserve chronological order and completeness of information were abandoned as the written tradition developed. The fourth evangelist, who was still working at his task in the last decade of the century and left it unfinished, recognised that a gospel could include only a small selection of the actions and sayings of Jesus' time on earth and did not feel constrained to preserve chronological order (e.g. in the placing of the Cleansing of the Temple).

In the Appendix to *Gospel Challenges*, two further theses were proposed and supported with arguments.

- St Luke's Acts of the Apostles is a revised and extended version of an earlier Acts (ending at

23:11), just as his Gospel is a revised and amplified version of St Mark's Gospel.

- This earlier Acts was written as a sequel, not to St Luke's Gospel, but to an earlier Gospel in which Jesus was with his disciples for forty days after his Resurrection, teaching them about the kingdom.

It is now suggested that this earlier text was the Gospel composed by M1, and an attempt will be made to reconstruct its forty-day Resurrection Narrative by first identifying the narratives that were retrojected by later evangelists. Then explanations will be given of why the later evangelists abbreviated the Forty-Day Resurrection Narrative and altered its geographical framework.

RETROJECTED NARRATIVES AND DISCOURSES

As was explained in *Gospel Challenges*, a number of stories and sayings that were originally parts of the Resurrection Narrative were, in the course of the written tradition, "retrojected" (thrown back) into the Narrative of the Galilean Ministry. The forty-day Resurrection Narrative can be reconstructed by identifying the retrojected items and replacing them in their original positions. The items in question are more numerous than the examples given in *Gospel Challenges*. It will be shown that the items listed below do not fit into the contexts in which they are found in canonical Matthew and would fit better into a post-Resurrection context. It does not necessarily follow that such items belonged to the original forty-day Resurrection Narrative – some of them may have been introduced later, by M2 or M3.

Parts of the Sermon on the Mount, Mt 5-7

Parts of the Sermon on the Mount do not fit into the opening phase of the Galilean ministry. It is inappropriate for Jesus to say to his disciples, before they have any understanding of him, "You are the salt of the earth...You are the light of the world" (Mt 5:13-14). In Mk 8:17-21 he becomes quite impatient with their lack of understanding or "hardness of heart". And long before he has given them any power or authority, it is inappropriate for him to warn them against saying to him: "Lord, Lord, in your name we prophesied; in your name we cast out demons, and in your name we did many miracles" (Mt 7:22). Nor is it likely that he said, "Do not think that I came to abolish the Law and the prophets; I came not to abolish but to fulfil," before anyone had accused him (or Paul) of trying to abolish the Law and the Prophets. The Sermon on the Mount, as it now stands, does not fit into its immediate context in canonical Matthew.

The Missionary Discourse, Mt 10:5-42

In the Missionary Discourse, Jesus predicts that his disciples will suffer persecution, that they will be put on trial, and that their preaching will cause the division of families (their own and others), but there is no evidence that any of these things happened during Jesus' Galilean ministry. "They returned to Jesus without meeting anything of what he had led them to expect."[7] Such things did happen after Pentecost. Clearly the discourse does not fit the context in which it is placed. It is much more relevant to the situation of the disciples in the post-Resurrection period.

Further, this discourse fits awkwardly just after Mt 9:38. The disciples are told to pray that God will send workers into the harvest just before they themselves are sent into the harvest. It seems that the evangelist (M2) who placed the Missionary Discourse here wished to show that prayers for harvesters did not go unheard (cf. below on Mt 16:28 and the immediately following Transfiguration). This discourse would fit much better into the post-Resurrection period, when Jesus is instructing his disciples about what they must do in the brief time of his absence. (Mt 10:23 was probably added by M2, who did not believe there was time for preaching to the Gentiles.)

Jesus' Thanksgiving to his Father, Mt 11:25-26

Jesus' exclamation of joy does not arise from anything in the preceding context in canonical Matthew. By its nature it ought to follow a scene in which the disciples have recognised something important that remains unknown to the public. It fits well after they have recognised Jesus as the Son of God, e.g. after the Walking on Water

(Mt 14:33), another retrojected text, as will be shown below.

(These sayings are probably more effective than the threats and promises in the conclusion of Mk 16:15-18 in sustaining the adherence of simple Christians to the Church today. The witness of miracles has ceased, and most Christians do not have time or training to scrutinise the reliability of the Gospels. They adhere to the Christian community because it gives them a sense of identity and of hope as members of a privileged in-group with a superior wisdom of its own.)

The Discussion about Parables, Mt 13:10-15

The discussion about Jesus' use of parables does not fit its context in canonical Matthew. The disciples cannot approach Jesus while he is teaching a crowd from the end of a boat. Nor does it arise naturally from the parable of the Sower that precedes it, since the Sower is not difficult to understand and does not conceal within it any of the "mysteries of the kingdom". If the mysteries include the extension of the Gospel to the Gentiles (Eph 3:9; Rom 16:25), this discussion about parables was probably not a part of M1 at all, neither of the Public Ministry nor of the Resurrection Narrative. It implies the outlook of M3.

The Feeding of the Five Thousand, Mt 14:13-21

In Mt 11:16-24, looking back over the ministry of the Baptist and over his own ministry so far, Jesus deplores the unresponsiveness of the Galileans, who are like sulking children sitting in the market-place refusing invitations to any sort of pastime. Between that passage and the Feeding of the Five Thousand occur the Beelzebul Dispute, the Rejection at Nazareth, and the Execution of the Baptist. Then suddenly, in the preamble to the Multiplication of Loaves and Fishes, we find that five thousand families have flocked to hear Jesus and have hung on his words for three days on end. Clearly the miracle does not fit its context. (In the Fourth Gospel, it is placed before the Bread of Life discourse, which is the turning-point after which the Galileans drift away from Jesus.) If the number was really five hundred, and the story has been improved in the telling, this may be the Appearance of Jesus "to five hundred at the same time," mentioned by St Paul in 1 Cor 15:6.

The Walking on Water, Mt 14:22-33

The story of the Walking on Water, which follows the Feeding of Five Thousand in Matthew, Mark and John, has all the characteristics of a post-Resurrection Appearance. Jesus appears unexpectedly, is taken for a ghost, reassures his disciples, and gives them proof of the reality of his body – in this case by enabling Peter too to walk on the water. At the end, Peter and the other disciples worship Jesus, saying: "Truly you are the Son of God" (14:33), which is out of place before Mt 16:17 where Peter makes the same confession of faith, and Jesus responds as if it were the result of a sudden revelation: "Blessed are you, Simon bar Jonah, because flesh and blood has not revealed it to you but my Father in heaven."

The Promise to Peter, Mt 16:17-19

The parallel text in Mark, which omits the Promise, develops much more smoothly. Jesus asks, "Who do you say that I am?" Peter replies, "You are the Messiah." Jesus does not praise him but proceeds at once to announce that the Son of Man (as he prefers to call himself) must suffer and die. Peter protests and is told he is a stumbling-block in Jesus' way. Then Jesus tells the disciples that they too must suffer (Mk 8:27-38). – Into this context, the Promise to Peter has been inserted, with the result that in Mt 16:17 Jesus pronounces Peter blessed as the recipient of a special revelation from the Father, and a minute later in 16:23 calls him "Satan". First Peter is called the Rock on which the Church will be built; then he is called a stumbling-block in Jesus' way. These are the results of the clumsy conflation of two distinct incidents.

Further, the disciples do not act differently towards Jesus after Mt 16:16-17, as they presumably would if they knew themselves to be in the presence of the Son of the living God.

The Call to Carry One's Cross, Mt 16:24-28

Jesus' appeal to his disciples to "take up their cross" and follow him is more likely to have been made after he has been crucified. This passage is probably a part of Jesus' post-Resurrection Missionary Discourse. It would follow smoothly after Mt 10:25.

The Transfiguration, Mt 17:1-8

The Question about Elijah (Mt 17:9-13) arises not from the Transfiguration but from Jesus' acceptance of the title "Messiah" in his dialogue with Peter (Mt 17:13-16). The disciples ask how can Jesus be Messiah if Elijah has not yet come, since Malachi 4:5 prophesies that Elijah must come first. Jesus replies that Elijah has come, in the person of John the Baptist, and they (the Jews) have ill-used him as they wished.[8] The story of the Transfiguration has been intruded into this context, between Peter's Confession of Jesus as Messiah and the question about Elijah, presumably to reveal the meaning of Peter's amplified Confession. As was shown in *Gospel Challenges*, pp. 57-59, by its nature the Transfiguration belongs after the Passion, not before it.

The Exorcism of an Epileptic Boy, Mt 17:14-20

As Bultmann pointed out, Jesus speaks here with unusual impatience, as if he were a visitor from another world and anxious to return there: "O unbelieving and perverse generation, how long shall I be with you? How long have I to endure you?"[9] This suggests a post-Resurrection context – which is not impossible if Jesus encountered large crowds of five hundred or more in Galilee in the forty-day Resurrection Narrative.

It may be significant that Jesus' reproach is addressed, not to Peter, James and John, who took the lead in the Church of Jerusalem, but to the rest of the "Twelve", who drop out of the story in the Acts of the Apostles. He tells them that if they had faith like a mustard seed, they could move mountains. (In most of the world's great religions, especially in India, faith has moved mountains of rock to build temples, but that is not exactly what Jesus meant.)

Instructions on Sin and Forgiveness, Mt 18:6-9, 15-22

In Mt 18 Jesus gives his disciples some instructions on the treatment of sin and sinners in the Church over which they will be rulers. These rules belong to the time when they understand that Jesus is about to leave them in charge of an organisation called the Church. But they do not understand that until after the Resurrection. Therefore the following passages must originally have been post-Resurrection instructions, formulated either by Jesus or by the disciples under the guidance of the Spirit.

Mt 18:6-9   On Scandals
Mt 18:15-17   On Treatment of Sinners
Mt 18:18   Jesus gives the disciples power to make rules.
Mt 18:19-20   On Absolution through Prayer
Mt 18:21-22   On Recidivists

In the Rules concerning the Treatment of Sinners, the teaching of the parable of the Lost Sheep is translated into precise regulations, written in a different style. These rules, inserted probably by

M2, were perhaps formulated in consequence of Peter's abrupt treatment of Ananias and Sapphira, to whom he gave no time for reflection or repentance and no opportunity to make amends (Acts 5:1-11).

If the correct text in Mt 18:15 is "If your brother sins against you," the admonition is addressed to all members of the Church: they should seek reconciliation privately and unobtrusively first. If the correct text is, "If your brother sins," the admonition is addressed to the pastor of a church. If he hears, for example, that a member of his congregation has rejected his wife and taken another woman, he is to speak to him first privately; then, if necessary, with two or three witnesses present; and if that too fails, the sinner is to be shunned "like a Gentile-or a tax-collector." This phrase implies that the regulations were formulated in very early days, before the Council of Jerusalem. They were probably known to Paul, who shows in his Epistle to the Galatians that before admonishing Peter publicly at Antioch (Gal 2:14), he spoke to him first privately (Gal 1:18), then in the presence of one or two witnesses (Gal 2:1).

A Lesson on Rulership, Mt 22:25-28

The Request of James and John (Mt 22:20-23) is for the first places, at Jesus' right and left, in the Messianic Banquet of the future kingdom. The added verses 25-28 are about the first places in the Church on earth. They belong to a context where the disciples understand that in future they will be rulers of the Christian community. Jesus warns them that they must not lord it over their subjects as Herod does.

Denunciation of the Scribes and Pharisees, Mt 23:1-15, 23-28

In canonical Matthew, Jesus, still in the temple, warns his disciples against abuses that may creep into the Church later. But at this point they have not been told that they will one day be rulers of Christian communities in the absence of Jesus. The denunciation does not fit the present context. Its placing in canonical Matthew has the unfortunate result of suggesting that Jesus provoked his arrest by unrestrained verbal attacks on the authorities.

The Lament over Jerusalem, Mt 23:37-39

The whole of this Lament is clearly out of place, but especially 23:39, "You will not see me again until you say, 'Blessed is he who comes in the name of the Lord.'" Placed where it is, this saying is not even true. The Jews of Jerusalem will see Jesus again, and they will cry out "Crucify him!" The Lament belongs to the very end of the post-Resurrection period, when Jesus looks back to Jerusalem before his Ascension and speaks of the future day when men will see him return as Judge, and will cry, some with joy, others with dread, "Blessed is he who comes in the name of the Lord."

The Eschatological Discourse, Mt 24:4-44

The Eschatological Discourse does not fit where it is placed in canonical Matthew, because the disciples have not yet been told that Jesus is going to leave them in charge of a community of believers while he is away in heaven with his Father, and that he will return one day in glory as the Judge of mankind. Nor are they in a position to understand at this point that when he returns they may have difficulty in recognising him and must therefore be careful to avoid following false claimants to Messiahship. They are certainly not told at this point that before he returns the temple will be desecrated and destroyed and the gospel will be preached to all nations. This discourse is clearly addressed to Christians who have never seen Christ and may be misled by false claimants to his title. It was probably written, by M1 or a contemporary prophet, in the panic atmosphere of the crisis caused by Caligula in AD 40-41,[10] and may have been introduced by M1 into some copies of his Resurrection Narrative, immediately after the angel's message following the Ascension:

> This Jesus who has been taken up from you into heaven will come in the same way as you saw him going into heaven.

In response, the men of Galilee might well ask their double question, "When will this be, and what will be the sign when the age will end?" The discourse then begins, appropriately, with a warning against being misled by false pretenders to the title of Messiah.

In the tense atmosphere of the crisis, the prophet makes two false predictions (Mk 13:14): the rebellion of the Jews will be provoked by a desecration of the temple, and when the war starts the Christians of Judea will flee to the hills. That is not what happened. (The prediction that the gospel must be preached to all nations before the end will come, Mk 13:10, is clearly an insertion made after the Council of Jerusalem.)

The Warning Parables, Mt 24:45-25:30

These parables warn the disciples, as future rulers of the Church, to be constantly vigilant, because Jesus will return suddenly to demand an account of their stewardship. They must not grow weary of waiting, saying, "My Master is long a-coming," and relax their standards of vigilance and service.

These parables were plainly not written to follow a Discourse in which the disciples were told that Jesus would not return until after the destruction of the temple and after the evangelisation of the whole world. They were written for a post-Resurrection context in which the disciples know that Jesus will leave them in charge of the Christian community while he is in heaven with his Father until the Day when he will return as Son of Man to judge all humankind.

(Note: the Judgment of the Nations, Mt 25: 31-46, is not addressed to the future rulers of the Church but to a much wider public. It talks of the future coming of the Son of Man but does not assume that the Christian community will be distinct from the Synagogue. It assumes, like the preaching of the Baptist, that the Day of Judgment will come soon. Jesus speaks of the coming of the Son of Man, but without identifying himself as the Son of Man.)

Jesus Comforts Peter, Lk 22:31-32

This word of comfort is probably a fragment of the narrative of the Appearance of Jesus to Peter mentioned in 1 Cor 15:5 and Lk 24:34.

> Simon, Simon,...I prayed for you that your faith might not fail. Now you go back (*epistrepsas*) and strengthen your brethren.

Replaced early in the post-Resurrection Narrative, the verb *epistrepho* has its normal meaning of returning to the place from which one came, here the room where the other disciples remain hidden behind closed doors. What else transpired at this meeting remains unknown, perhaps because Jesus enjoined silence.

The Resurrection Narrative of M1

After identifying the retrojected passages and excluding those that appear to be later additions to the written tradition (i.e. to represent the views of M2 and M3), it is possible to make a conjectural reconstruction of the Resurrection Narrative of M1 by returning the displaced passages to where they came from. It transpires that in M1 Jesus appeared to his disciples on about eleven occasions, sometimes as much as seven days apart. If he had appeared only once, the disciples might have told themselves later that it was only a dream, but after repeated Appearances, in some of which Jesus gave them instructions or performed a miracle or exorcism, they could no longer doubt or relapse into the uncertainty of "wondering." After the Feeding of the Five Thousand, when they were left with twelve baskets of fragments, they could not doubt that the miracle had actually happened.[11]

RECONSTRUCTION:
from the Empty Tomb to Pentecost

Day 1 Easter Sunday   *Mt 28:1-8*

The women discover the Empty Tomb. An angel tells them that Jesus is risen and the disciples will see him in Galilee. They report to the disciples, who do not believe them. Peter goes to investigate, and comes away wondering – half-believing. Jesus appears to him, comforts him, sends him back to confirm his brothers, and sets out for a nearby *komopolis*.

Jesus appears to two disciples on the road to Emmaus and spends much of the day with them. When he disappears, they return to Jerusalem and report to the other disciples, and are told that Peter says he has seen Jesus.

Late in the evening, Jesus appears to the disciples (all except Thomas), reproaches them for being so slow to believe (Mk 16:14), forgives them, gives them power to forgive others (Jn 20:23), and gives rules for forgiveness (Mt 18:1-5; 18:10-14; 15-20; 21-22). He then repeats the order he gave through the angel: they are to leave for Galilee to meet him on a certain day at a certain mountain.[12]

Day 2   *Mt 28:16*

Probably the next day, the disciples set out for Galilee to meet Jesus on the day and the mountain he has specified.

Day 8   *Jn 20:24-29*

Unexpectedly, Jesus appears to his disciples, who are now in Galilee, once again behind closed doors though not for fear of the Jews, this time with Thomas present. He convinces Thomas of the reality of his Resurrection and pronounces blessed those who believe in him without having seen him risen.

Days 8-9   *Jn 21:1-19*

Peter and six others go fishing at night. Jesus appears unexpectedly at dawn, gives them a miraculous catch, eats breakfast with them, gives Peter the opportunity to cancel his three denials by a threefold profession of love, and appoints him Shepherd of the whole flock.

Jesus commissions his disciples to go out two by two to preach, to exorcise, and to heal, but in Galilee and Judea only. He also warns the disciples of persecutions and trials to come (Mt 10:1,5b-22; Mt 16:24-28; Mt 10: 26-42).

Rumour spreads among the people of Galilee that Jesus is risen and will be seen on the mountain. Those who believe, about five hundred in number, get up and go to see him. (Both in the Infancy and in the Resurrection Narratives, those who believe get up and go; those who do not, remain where they are.)

Days 14-15-16-17   Mt 17:1-8, 14-20; Mt 5-7

On the appointed day, the disciples go to the mountain and find a crowd assembled. In the evening, Jesus appears, takes Peter and two other disciples apart by themselves, and is transfigured before them. He is seen conversing with Moses and Elijah; they disappear, and a Voice from heaven declares, "This is my beloved Son, in whom I am well pleased; hear him!"

On the following morning, when they come down the mountain, Jesus exorcises the Epileptic Boy. He and the disciples are met by a large crowd (Lk 9:37), in the presence of which Jesus gives his disciples the Sermon on the Plain (original version[13]).

Day 17 *Mk 6:30-44*

In the evening, Jesus makes the people sit down in groups of fifty and a hundred, each supervised by a disciple, and multiplies loaves and fishes to feed the multitude.

Days 17-18 *Mt 14:22-33; Mt 11:25-26*

During the night, Jesus appears walking on the water; to convince the disciples that they are not seeing a ghost, he allows Peter too to walk on the water. The men in the boat then confess Jesus as Son of God. Jesus thanks his Father for revealing these things to the simple. Then he tells them to return two by two to Jerusalem, where they will see him on an appointed day. Next day, they set out for Jerusalem.

Day 25 *Lk 22:24-30*

Back in Jerusalem, the disciples meet for supper, and Jesus bequeaths to them his kingdom, which they must rule in his absence. He warns them against ambition for positions of eminence and tells them they must not rule like Herod (Mt 20:24-28), or like the scribes and Pharisees, whom he denounces in a series of Woes (Mt 23:4-28).

Day 31 *Mt 25:1-30*

Jesus gives his disciples a number of parables warning them to be ever watchful, since the Son of Man will return unexpectedly, they will never know when.

Day 38   *Acts 1:6-11*

Jesus and the disciples assemble for a Last Supper, after which he leads them out to Bethany. He looks back and utters his lament over Jerusalem (Mt 23:37-39), then blesses his disciples, tells them to remain in Jerusalem to await the coming of the Spirit, and, unexpectedly, ascends into heaven in glory accompanied by angels. An angel tells the disciples that Jesus will return as they have seen him go.

Day 50, Pentecost

The disciples are baptised with the Holy Spirit. Peter, animated by the Spirit of Jesus, makes a powerful speech, inveighing against those who called for the crucifixion of Jesus. He announces the Resurrection of Jesus and offers forgiveness and baptism in his name to the inhabitants of Jerusalem. Three thousand accept his offer.

***

In his Galilean Narrative, M1 collected a number of stories that point forward to the events of his Resurrection Narrative. The order of these Anticipations was upset by M2 and M3 who fitted them into patterns of their own design. Probably the matching began a little earlier, namely, from the moment of Jesus' death, thus:

Cure of Centurion's Servant, Mt 8:5-10, Jn 4:46-53	Centurion's Confession, Mt 27:54

The officer in the earlier text recognises Jesus' power to cause miracles at a distance (this is still clearer in the parallel text, Jn 4:46-53, where Jesus at Cana causes the miracle to occur at Capharnaum). In the later text, the centurion recognises in the earthquake and breaking of rocks the effect of Jesus' final act of will, as he dies.

Peter's Wife's Mother and
Healing of Many (Isa 54:3), Mt 8:14-17   Women on Calvary, Mt 27:55

In the earlier passage a woman related to one of the disciples is cured and begins to minister to Jesus in Galilee. In the later passage many women who have come up from Galilee stand waiting to minister to Jesus. Two of them are mothers of his disciples. The other is Mary Magdalene whom Jesus had cured (cf. Mk 16:9).

Would-be Followers, Mt 8:18-22   Burial of Jesus in another man's
tomb by pious Jews, Mt 27:57-61

Jesus' replies to the two would-be disciples are prophetic of his deposition and burial. If the first of them believes that Jesus will end up in a royal palace, that will explain Jesus' imagery. Herod the fox has his lair, and the Roman eagle his nest, but the Son of Man has no resting-place on earth. He is born in another man's stable and buried in another man's tomb.

The second would-be disciple probably means: "Let me go home and provide for my father till he dies (in obedience to the fourth commandment)." Jesus' response appears to imply that the petitioner is the only one of his family who believes. The burial of the unbelieving father can be left to his unbelieving kindred. Jesus appears to have held that the call to preach the Gospel overrides all obligations to one's parents, whether they believe or not (cf. Mt 4:22). As time went on, later evangelists may have seen here an application of the wider principle that religious obligation can override moral obligation, the classic example of which is Abraham preparing to kill his son at God's command. They may have concluded that converting sinners is more important than preserving the historical accuracy of the Gospel story.

GALILEAN ANTICIPATIONS OF THE RESURRECTION NARRATIVE OF M1

Gadarene Exorcism, Mt 8:28-34; Mk 5:1-13

Discovery of Empty Tomb, Mt 28:1-8 [Mt 28:9-10 added by M4]

The women going to the tomb expect to see the battered and bruised body of Jesus; instead, they find that no bonds could hold him – he has escaped and gone. The destruction of the herd of swine prefigures the overthrow of the powers of evil by the Resurrection and Glorification of Jesus. (Gadara was the home of one Philodemus, who a century before Jesus' time left Gadara to pursue a distinguished career as an Epicurean philosopher in Rome. If the Gadarenes were Epicureans, Jesus' teaching would be particularly uncongenial to them. An Epicurean could describe himself, ironically, as "a pig from Epicurus' sty."[14])

Herdsmen flee to city, Mk 5:14-17

Guards flee to city, Mt 28:11-15

The flight of the herdsmen into the city in the earlier text prefigures the flight of the guards into Jerusalem in the later. In neither case does the report of what has happened bring the hearers to faith in Jesus. The Gadarenes' request that Jesus leave their territory prefigures the rejection of the apostolic Gospel by the rulers of Jerusalem.

At Mt 28:11, M1's text probably said: "Some of the guards… reported to the chief priests what had happened" or "what they had seen and heard" (not "all that had happened"). In 28:4 they are knocked senseless by the earthquake so that they do not witness anything that happens in 28:5-10. In the Gadarene story, the herdsmen report only what has happened to the pigs.

Cured Man sent home, Mk 5:18-20   Peter searches for Jesus, Jn 20:3-10
Peter searches for Jesus, Mk 1:35-38

At the end of the Gadarene story, the cured demoniac asks to be allowed to stay with Jesus, but Jesus tells him to go home and tell how "the Lord" has had pity on him. This may well be an anticipation of the lost appearance to Peter. It suggests a scene in which Jesus casts the demon of timidity out of Peter, forgives him, and sends him to speak to the other disciples about the Lord's mercy.

The brief story in Mk 1:35-38 has little meaning except as an anticipation of Peter's later search for Jesus; see above (p. 20). St Matthew omitted it, either because he intended to omit the later text or because he did not see the connection.

Jairus's Daughter & Two Blind Men,   Journey to Emmaus, Lk 24:13-35
Mt 9:18-31; Mk 5:21-43

The Markan version of the Jairus story is fuller and offers more links with the Resurrection narrative; as often, Mark preserves the original text of M1 more faithfully than canonical Matthew. In both incidents, Jesus is going along with his disciples towards a house, and as they go, there is a discussion of the faith of certain believing women. In both narratives there is a point where they stop on the journey: in Mk 5:30 Jesus turns round to look for the woman who has touched him, and the disciples expostulate with him; so too in Lk 24:17-18 the disciples stand still in amazement, and again they expostulate with Jesus. They mock him for not knowing what has been going on in Jerusalem during the last few days: if he doesn't know what has happened, he is the only person in Jerusalem who doesn't! Similarly in the courtyard of Jairus's house in Mk 5:40 Jesus is ironically mocked for not knowing that the child is dead. There is also the obvious connection that the Raising of Jairus's Daughter is a Resurrection miracle. Not everyone is allowed to see the raising of the girl in Galilee: the chosen witnesses are Peter, James, John and the parents – just as only chosen witnesses see Jesus after his Resurrection. Mark alone supplies the name "Jairus", which means in Hebrew "He will raise", and Mark alone says that after raising the girl, Jesus suggested that she be given something to eat. The Emmaus incident too ends with a meal.[15]

The structural link between the earlier and the later passage here explains how the Cure of the Woman comes to be inserted within the Raising of Jairus's Daughter: the arrangement was not made by a preacher in the "oral" period but by the evangelist who created this elaborate literary structure.[16]

A further reason why it was fitting to sandwich the one story within the other is that in both of them what Jesus says sounds incredible and provokes mockery but turns out to be right: in the midst of a throng he can recognise the touch of faith, and death to him is a sleep from which the sleeper can arise. The combination also shows that Jesus responds to the petitions both of the powerful and of the powerless. The main miracle should also prepare the chosen disciples, Peter, James and John, for Jesus' own Resurrection, but to judge from the Resurrection narratives the disciples did not profit by this lesson. (Jairus's daughter is twelve years old and the woman has suffered her internal malady for twelve years. These details help to link the stories together but do not explain the sandwich construction.)

During the meal at the end of the Emmaus narrative Jesus opens the eyes of the two travellers. Immediately after the Jairus story he cures two blind men. In both narratives he does so inside a house (Mt 9:28 makes a point of this). The phrase "their eyes were opened" (Mt 9:30) is repeated almost exactly in Lk 24:30. Further, Jesus shows a curious sign of impatience with the blind men in Mt 9:30, just as he reproaches the two disciples on the road to Emmaus in Lk 24:25, "O foolish and slow of heart!" Finally, in Mt 9:31 the cured men at once tell other people what has happened, just as the disciples whose eyes are opened at Emmaus hasten back to Jerusalem to tell the other disciples.

Healing of Two Blind Men, Mt 9:27-31

The Appearance to Peter, Lk 26:34

The Appearance of Jesus to Peter is merely mentioned, not narrated, at the end of the Emmaus narrative, without any indication of where it took place, or of what was said. It seems safe to say that if any of the evangelists had known the details, he would have described this Appearance. Perhaps the details (apart from Lk 22:31-32?) were unknown because Peter refused to divulge them, having been told by Jesus to keep the matter secret. It so happens that in the Galilean anticipation, the Healing of Two Blind Men (Mt 9:27-31), Jesus says to the men, "See that no one knows." This order is not obeyed by the blind men. It is perhaps more applicable to the Appearance to Peter, just as Isa 53:4, quoted in Mt 8:17, is more applicable to the death and deposition of Jesus than to the context in Mt 8.

Stilling of Tempest,[17] Mt 8:23-27
Cure of Paralytic, Mt 9:1-6
Calling of Matthew,
Eating with Sinners, Mt 9:9-13

Sulky Children, Mt 11:16-19

Appearance to Ten Disciples in Jerusalem, Mk 16:14; Jn 20:19-23; Lk 24:36-49; Acts 10:42

Return to Galilee, Mt 28:16
Appearance to Thomas, Jn 20:24-29

There is a notable contrast here between the detailed narratives of the Galilean incidents and the terseness of the corresponding Resurrection Narrative, where in rapid succession Jesus convinces the disciples of his identity, commissions them, gives them the Holy Spirit, and empowers them to forgive sins. Why, one wonders, are such important matters dealt with so briefly? But the real problem here is, Why is Jn 20:19-23 so concise whereas the narratives that precede and follow it (20:11-18 and 21:1-23) are so diffuse? A possible explanation is that Jn 20:19-23, which is similar in style to the condensed narrative of Mk 16:9-13, may be an abbreviated version of a much longer narrative, which, regrettably, the fourth evangelist did not choose to preserve. It may well have been as diffuse as the Raising of Lazarus, with which it has certain links (e.g. between 11:44 and 20:23, and Thomas is doubting Thomas on both occasions). It probably clarified the connection between the items compressed into 20:21-23, showing that Jesus first made peace with the disciples by forgiving them for their desertion of him in the crisis, then commissioned them, saying: "As my Father has sent me to forgive you, so I send you to forgive the sins of others." Then he breathed upon them, re-creating them (Gen 2:7) and empowering them to communicate his Spirit to repentant sinners. Then he made explicit that the power to forgive or not to forgive lay within their own decision. The most appropriate time for him to give them power to forgive was when they had just experienced forgiveness and reconciliation themselves.

As for the Galilean anticipations, in the Stilling of the Tempest, the disciples believe themselves in danger of death while Jesus lies asleep. They panic and wake him roughly, crying "Don't you care?" He rises up, creates calm, and rebukes them for lack of courage and lack of faith. In the matching Resurrection Appearance, the Risen Jesus again rebukes their lack of faith (Mk 16:14), then forgives their defection during his passion, gives them power to forgive the sins of others, and breathes his Spirit into them to strengthen them. Metaphorically he pours new wine into the new skins.

In the Cure of a Paralytic Jesus reveals his power to forgive sins; in the Appearance to the Disciples he communicates the same power to them. Other links between these matching scenes are that in each Jesus offers proof to overcome incredulity; both are concerned with seeing-and-believing. In Mk 2:7 the scribes ask, "Who can forgive sins but God alone?" – which points forward to Thomas's confession, "My Lord and my God!" Further the Cure of the Paralytic is described as a Resurrection. Jesus says, "Rise up!" and, says the evangelist, "He rose up." And in Mk 2:6-8 Jesus reveals his knowledge of men's secret thoughts, just as in Jn 20:27-28 he reveals that he knows what Thomas said in his absence.

The parable of the Sulky Children, which is poorly placed in canonical Matthew (11:16-19), fits extremely well after the Calling of Matthew. The Pharisees who disapproved of John's asceticism now disapprove of Jesus' eating with sinners. They hold aloof from both John and Jesus, like sulky children who refuse to take part in other children's games of any kind. In the later column Thomas adopts a similar attitude: when the other disciples are rejoicing over Jesus' Resurrection, he refuses to believe and persists in his gloom.

The Pharisees' observation on Jesus' eating and drinking with sinners may originally have pointed forward to a Resurrection Appearance in which Jesus shared a normal meal with his disciples. Peter refers to such occasions in his speech to Cornelius when he says, "We ate and drank with him after his rising from the dead" (Acts 10:42).

The Question about Fasting enables Jesus to explain that his teaching is different from the teachings of the Baptist and of the Pharisees. The wine is the new teaching, invested with power (Mk 1:27); the new bottles are men like Matthew. St Paul comments on these new bottles in Gal 2:6: "What they once were makes no difference to me; God is no respecter of persons."

Miraculous Catch, Lk 5:1-11 Appearance at Lakeside, Jn 21:1-19
Compassion of Jesus, 9:35-38 Miraculous Catch; Peter made Shepherd
Calling of Twelve, (Mt 10:1-4) Lk 6:12-16

In Mt 9:35-38, Jesus sees the common people as a flock of sheep in need of a shepherd. After a night of prayer, he selects the Twelve. In the later text, he takes compassion on the disciples who have laboured all night and caught nothing; then he appoints Peter shepherd of his whole flock.

The Gospels do not allow us to see what were Jesus' remoter intentions when he called the Twelve. Immediately, they were chosen to help shepherd the sheep of the house of Israel. After the Resurrection, when Jesus' horizon was extended universally, he chose a man of quite a different type for his apostle to the Gentiles.

Offer of an Easy Yoke, Mt 11:28-30 Missionary Discourse, Mt 10:5-42
Dispute in Cornfields, Mt 12:1-7 + Mt 16:24-28
Cure of Withered Hand, Mt 12:9-14
Mother & Brothers of Jesus, Mt 12:46-50

In the Missionary Discourse, Jesus is particularly concerned that his missionary disciples should not become a burden or vexation to the common people, as are the Pharisees in the earlier texts. He is offering the people an Easy Yoke, not a fresh burden. Further, he expects his disciples to separate themselves from their birth families, as he has done himself, now that they are members of the new family based on faith. From Mt 10:23 they form the impression that they should restrict their missionary journeys to the land of Israel.

| The Baptist's Question, Mt 11:2-11 | Appearance on Mountain, and Transfiguration, Mt 17:1-8[18] |

In the later scene, heaven itself answers the Baptist's question, by repeating in the same words the revelation given to John at the baptism of Jesus. (To judge from 2 Pet 1:16-19, Peter in his later years looked back to the Transfiguration rather than to the healing miracles as the ground of his faith in Jesus. Similarly Paul based his apologetic on his Damascus vision rather than on the events of Jesus' ministry.)

| The Beelzebul Dispute, Mt 12:22-32 | Exorcism of Epileptic Boy, Mt 17:14-20 |

The accusation made in the Beelzebul Dispute, that Jesus is an agent or tool of Beelzebul, is definitively refuted by the Voice from heaven in the Transfiguration together with Jesus' exorcism of a particularly stubborn demon as he descends from the mountain with his brow still reflecting the divine glory (Mk 9:14).

The Canaanite Woman, Feeding of Five Thousand,
Mt 15:21-28 Mk 6:30-44

In the earlier text Jesus declares that he is sent only to the lost sheep of the house of Israel and allows himself to be coaxed into granting a few crumbs from the children's table to a witty Gentile woman. In the later text he provides a superabundance of food for the children of Israel.

Caesarea Philippi, Mk 8:27-33 Walking on Water, Mt 14:22-33
 Jesus' Thanksgiving, Mt 11:25-27

Peter distinguishes himself in both scenes. In the earlier, Jesus is recognised as Messiah; in the later, as the Son of God; then Jesus gives thanks that these things have been revealed to the simple.

Following Jesus, Mk 8:31-38 Promise of Twelve Thrones, Lk 22:28-30
 <Announcement about the Future>

At this point in the Resurrection Narrative, Jesus informs his disciples that the time will soon come when they will be left in charge of those who believe and are baptised, while he himself will be seated at the right hand of God, awaiting his return at an unknown date, for which they must always be ready.

 <Return to Jerusalem>
Execution of the Baptist, Request of James and John,
at Herod's Banquet, Mk 6:14-29 Mt 20:20-22, 23b-28

For Herod's Banquet in particular, Mark preserves the original text of M1 more faithfully than Matthew. On its links with the Request of James and John, see *Gospel Challenges*, p. 73.

The Sower, the Seed growing Secretly,   Warning Parables,
Mk 4:1-9, 26-29   Mt 24:36-25:30

The agricultural parables of the earlier collection emphasise the powers inherent in the word itself and in the earth that receives it. The later group of parables shows that the earlier ones do not imply that pastoral care will be superfluous. The disciples will be not only sowers of seed but prudent stewards and householders.

Woes over Unrepentant Cities   Woes over Scribes and Pharisees, Mt 23:2-15
No Ascension for Capharnaum,   Lament over Jerusalem, Mt 23:37-39
Mt 11:20-24   Ascension of Jesus, Acts 1:4-11

In the earlier passage Jesus borrows the imagery of Isaiah 14:13-15.

> You said in your heart,
>   'I will ascend to heaven;
> above the stars of God
>   I will set my throne on high....
> I will ascend about the heights of the clouds,
>   I will make myself like the Most High.'
> But you are brought down to Sheol,
>   to the depths of the Pit.

The imagery of the Lament (23:37) is drawn from Psalm 36:7-9, which Jesus takes as addressed to him, not by him to God.

> How precious is thy steadfast love, O God!
>   The children of men take refuge in the
>   shadow of thy wings.
> They feast on the abundance of thy house,
>   and thou givest them drink from the river of
>   thy delights.
> For with thee is the fountain of life;
>   in thy light do we see light.

It is a fitting prayer for the children of the new Jerusalem to address to him.

After the Ascension, M1 probably continued further, to round off the story with the fulfilment of John the Baptist's prophecy of Spirit-Baptism. The ending of M1 matched the beginning, something like this:

Promise of Spirit Baptism, Mt 3:11-12	Jesus quotes John's Promise, Acts 1:4-5
Jesus is anointed King at his Baptism Mt 3:13-17; Lk 3:21-22	Question about the Kingdom, Acts 1:6
(Psalm 2:7, quoted by the Voice in Lk 3:22, is taken from an enthronement psalm.)	
Temptation in the Desert, Mk 1:12-13[19]	Ascension, Acts 1:9-10
	<Eschatological Discourse, Mk 13:4-36>
Prophecy of Isaiah, Mt 4:18-22	Prophecy of Jesus' Return, Acts 1:11
Calling of First Disciples, Mt 4:18-22	List of Apostles, Acts 1:13-14
Numerous Miracles[20], Mt 4:23-24	Coming of the Spirit, Acts 2:1-4
Crowds from afar, Mt 4:25	Crowds from afar, Acts 2:5-13
Repent or Perish, Lk 13:1-9	Peter's Speech at Pentecost, Acts 2:14-34

THE EXPECTATIONS OF THE DISCIPLES AFTER PENTECOST

In the parable of the Wicked Tenants Jesus indicated that authority would be taken away from the Sadducees and Pharisees and given to his disciples; he did not suggest that the disciples would rule or preside over only a small segment of the Jewish population. Either Jesus himself did not know how the future would unfold (Acts 1:7; Mk 14:32), or he deliberately left the disciples in uncertainty to respond to the situation as it might develop. After the Ascension and Pentecost they understood that Jesus had left them to preach and to organise churches in Israel until a day in the not distant future when he would return as Judge (Mt 10:23), probably before the death of the last apostle (Mt 16:28; Jn 21:22).

Then came the crisis under Caligula in AD 40-41, when a Jewish-Christian prophet[21] thought he could see the future more clearly and expressed his vision in the Eschatological Discourse: the temple would be desecrated; there would be war with Rome; the Christian community would flee to the mountains; Jerusalem would fall; some time after that Christ would return. But this vision was really no great help. The emperor's statue was not set up in the temple; the community fled to Pella, below sea level; Jerusalem fell, and the delay of the Parousia went on and on and on.

***

Next, what preceded this Galilean Chain, and what followed it? What preceded it was a parallelism linking the ministry of the Baptist to the inauguration of Jesus ministry.

John in the desert, Mt 3:1	Jesus in the desert, Mk 1:12-13 (Mt 4:1-12)
Repent for the kingdom, Mt 3:2	Prophecy of Isaiah, Mt 4:13-16
Prophecy of Isaiah, Mt 3:3	Repent for the kingdom, Mt 4:17
John's Clothing and Diet, Mt 3:4 (Elijah typology)	Call of First Disciples, Mt 4:18-22 (Elijah typology)
People flock to John, Mt 3:5-6	People flock to Jesus, Mt 4:23-25
Preaching of John, Mt 3:7-12; Lk 3:10-13	Jesus warns the crowds, Lk 13:1-9[22]

What followed the Galilean Chain in M1? After pronouncing the Woes over the Unrepentant Cities of Galilee (Mt 11:20-24), Jesus immediately left Galilee (Mt 19:1) and made the journey to Jerusalem. M1 related no incident till Jesus arrived in Jericho, where he encountered Zacchaeus and lodged with him, and healed the blind Bartimaeus. He then made his Triumphal Entry into Jerusalem, and from that point on as far as the Burial of Jesus M1's narrative included most of the incidents that are preserved, with little alteration, in Matthew, Mark and Luke.

Geographical Note

In M1, the geographical pattern of the Resurrection Narrative was similar to the geographical pattern of the Public Ministry: a beginning in the south, outside Jerusalem, a journey north, a reunion in Galilee, miracles and discourses in Galilee, and a return to Jerusalem for the "raising up" of Jesus. Which pattern was modelled on the other is hard to say.

M2's Revision of the Work of M1

If M2 wrote about 45-49 AD, some ten years after M1, he will have known about the following events:

- the Conversion of Cornelius and Peter's Report in Jerusalem
- the Conversion of certain Samaritans, with the cooperation of Peter and John
- the Persecution of Christians by Saul/Paul
  the Conversion of Saul/Paul
- the creation of a mixed church of Jews and Gentiles at Antioch
- the sending-out of a Gentile mission from Antioch
- the successful Missionary Journey of Barnabas and Paul.

Not all of the brethren in Jerusalem approved of these developments. According to Acts 15:1, there were still some who believed that Gentile converts needed to be told that "Unless you are circumcised [and live?] according to the custom of Moses, you cannot be saved."[23] M2 himself shared this view and designed his Gospel accordingly.

It was not an unreasonable position. Those who held it understood John the Baptist to have told his disciples and the public (Jn 6:14) that Jesus was the *Erchomenos*, the Greater One who was to come after him, to give the final interpretation of the Law (Deut 18:15) and later to apply the Law as Judge of all Mankind. It was therefore to be expected that Jesus would give his moral teaching, as he did, in the form of commentary on the Law, revealing the full requirements of the spirit of the Law, and it was a reasonable corollary that all Christians, including any who were of Gentile origin, must be taught to obey the Law as interpreted by Jesus.

In the view of M2, Jesus had told his disciples not to go and preach to the Gentiles (Mt 10:5). The Son of Man would come even before they had finished their task in Israel (Mt 10:23). He had given his apostles no instructions on the questions that were bound to arise if they went beyond Israel and preached to other nations: When Gentiles accept the Gospel, are they to be circumcised? Are they to observe the whole of the Law? Are they to observe the Sabbath, for example, and the rest of the Jewish calendar? Can Jewish disciples share meals with them, and intermarry with them? Are Gentile believers to be regarded as second-class citizens, like the "God-fearers" (Acts 13:26) attached to the synagogues of the Diaspora? – and so on. If Jesus meant his disciples to go to the Gentiles, would he not have instructed them on these matters? Another consideration was that none of the Twelve had initiated a Gentile mission. The pioneering work in Samaria, Syria (Antioch), Cyprus, Asia Minor, Caesarea, was not done by any of the Twelve.

When Peter arrived back in Jerusalem after the conversion of Cornelius, his Jewish critics complained: "You lodged with uncircumcised men and ate with them." Peter replied that he did this in obedience to a vision, and in the continuation of his discourse justified his baptising the Gentile household. (Circumcision is not mentioned, but Peter means: baptising them without circumcising them.) His hearers fell silent, raised no further objection, and glorified God saying, "Then to the Gentiles too God has granted repentance unto life" (11:18). But clearly not all were convinced that the conversion of Cornelius established a universal rule. Peter himself did not launch a mission to the Gentiles. According to Paul, he agreed to confine his efforts to the Jews (Gal 2:9). The debate over the necessity of circumcision for Gentile converts continued for years.

The evangelisation of Samaria was initiated by Philip the deacon. When Christians left Jerusalem to escape from Saul's persecution, Philip went to Samaria and started preaching there, on his own initiative. When the apostles in Jerusalem heard of what he had done, they sent Peter and John to pray for the converts and lay-on hands, conferring the gift of the Holy Spirit. M2 can hardly have approved of this, since he believed that Jesus had said to his disciples, "Enter no town of the Samaritans," and previously the "apostles" resident in Jerusalem had observed this restriction.

When M2 heard of the conversion of Paul, he probably suspected it was a trick to enable Paul to discover the whereabouts of the leaders of the Church. Peter himself appears to have shared this suspicion, since he needed persuasion by Barnabas before he would grant Paul an interview (Acts 9:26-27). When Paul started preaching in Jerusalem and stirring up controversy, no doubt M2 was glad to see him packed off to Tarsus, for his own good as well as for the peace of the Church (Acts 9:30).

Again, the establishment of the first mixed church of Gentiles and Jews at Antioch was not initiated by the apostles in Jerusalem, but by certain Greek-speaking Jews from Cyprus and Cyrene (11:9). When news of this reached Jerusalem, Barnabas was sent to investigate. He approved of what had been done and called in Paul to help. Once again, M2 was probably dismayed at this development. The expansion of the Church seemed to have escaped from the hands of Jesus' chosen apostles, who were simply following in the wake of events and approving the *faits accomplis* of others.

Next it was reported that the Holy Spirit had intervened in the church of Antioch (12:2) – not of Jerusalem! – to initiate a mission into Cyprus, Pamphilia, Pisidia, and heaven knows where else, and that the missionaries were baptising Gentile converts without circumcising them. Some of the conservatives of Jerusalem, including M2, thought this was a mistake. John Mark, who refused to go into Pisidia, may have thought the same (13:13). When Paul and Barnabas returned to Antioch, a deputation of these conservatives was waiting for them, teaching the Christians of Antioch that "unless a man is circumcised according to the custom of Moses, he cannot be saved." M2 is a Gospel written from the conservative point of view in this situation, shortly before the matter was referred to the Council at Jerusalem.

M2 had undoubtedly heard that Paul, the

former persecutor of the Church, was travelling among the Gentiles, telling them that the death of Christ was the end of the Law, that the Law of Moses was a temporary measure imposed on the chosen people till in the fullness of time Israel should achieve maturity. He may have heard rumours that Paul was telling Jews of the Diaspora not to circumcise their children (Acts 21:21). Like many others, he probably understood Paul to be saying that Jesus came to abolish the Law and establish a new regime of grace (Rom 6:14). He was one of those who disapproved of Paul's missionary activity and disagreed with his theology (cf. Acts 15:1). In M2's view, Jesus came to reform Judaism from within, not to create a new religion on the ruins of the old. He was sent only to the lost sheep of the house of Israel, and his mission was to fulfil the Law, by revealing its full demands, not to destroy it. His disciples too were sent to the lost sheep of Israel, not to the Gentiles.

M2 accordingly amplified the Sermon on the Plain into the Sermon on the Mount and transferred it from the post-Resurrection period to the early Galilean ministry. Close to the beginning of the Sermon he inserted a formal statement of Jesus' attitude to the Law: "Till heaven and earth pass away, no jot or tittle of the Law shall pass away." Then, in the Antitheses, he showed that Jesus gave much of his moral teaching in the form of commentary on the Law, revealing the insufficiency of contemporary Pharisaic interpretations.

In his collection of parables, M2 inserted the parable of the Weeds, an extension of the imagery of the Sower, in which the enemy sower is Paul, sowing the false doctrine of Lawlessness (*anomia*). In the middle of this allegorical parable, the Lord's servants (Peter, James and John), by asking the Lord what is to be done, give their Master the opportunity to pass judgment: "An enemy has done this."

In the Syro-Phoenician incident, M2 makes Jesus explicitly affirm that he is sent only to the lost sheep of the house of Israel, and at the beginning of the Missionary Discourse, retrojected into the Galilean ministry, he makes Jesus impose the same restriction upon his disciples. He regards the instructions given in his amplified Missionary Discourse as valid for all time, not cancelled out in any post-Resurrection Appearance.

In his denunciation of the Pharisees, Jesus is made to condemn Pharisees who scour sea and land to make one proselyte and then make him twice as much a son of hell as they are themselves (Mt 23:15). No one is named, but the cap fits Paul. Undoubtedly Paul was misunderstood by Christian Jews of Jerusalem, who tried to lynch him when he went there with alms in AD 58.

THE RESURRECTION NARRATIVE OF M2:
from the Empty Tomb to the Ascension

M2 wished, therefore, to show Christianity as a movement of reform developing within the heartland of Judaism, namely Jerusalem, in fulfilment of the prophecy of Isaiah that in the latter days,

"Out of Zion shall go forth the law, and the Word of the Lord from Jerusalem" (Is 2:4). Accordingly, he decided to omit from his Resurrection Narrative the return to Galilee and the Appearances in Galilee, and to salvage these Galilean stories and Discourses by retrojecting them into the public ministry of Jesus. Nevertheless he retained M1's series of Galilean Anticipations of the Death and Resurrection Narratives, including those which pointed forward to the events he had displaced. He renounced any attempt to keep the incidents and Discourses in chronological order. Here is what he was left with:

<Sermon on the Mount, Mt 5-7>

<Cure of a Leper, Mt 8:1-4>[24]

Cure of Centurion's Servant, Mt 8:5-11	Centurion's Confession, Mt 27:54
Peter's Wife's Mother, etc., Mt 8:14-17	Women on Calvary, Mt 27:55-56
Would-be Followers, Mt 8:18-22	Burial of Jesus, Mt 27:57-61
The Gadarene Exorcism, Mk 5:1-13	Discovery of the Empty Tomb, Mt 28:1-8
Herdsmen flee to city, Mk 5:14-17 Cured Man is sent home, Mk 5:18-20	Guards flee to City, Mt 28:11-15
Peter searches for Jesus, Mk 1:35-38	Jesus appears to Peter, Lk 22:31-32
Jairus's Daughter & Cure of Two Blind Men, Mt 9:18-31	Journey to Emmaus, Lk 24:13-35
Stilling of Tempest, Mt 8:23-27 Cure of Paralytic, Mt 9:1-6 Eating with Sinners, Mt 9:9-13	Appearance to (10) Disciples in Jerusalem, Jn 20:19-23; Lk 24:36-46[47]48-49
Sulky Children, Mt 11:16-19	
Miraculous Catch, Lk 5:1-11	
Compassion of Jesus, Mt 9:35-38 Offer of an Easy Yoke, Mt 11:28-30 Dispute in Cornfields, Mt 12:1-7 Cure of Withered Hand, Mt 129-14	[Missionary Discourse, Mt 10:5-42, retrojected]
Mother & Brothers of Jesus, Mt 12:46-50	
The Baptist's Question, Mt 11:2-11	

The Beelzebul Dispute, Mt 12:22-32

[SP amplified into SM and retrojected, as above]

The Canaanite Woman, Mt 15:21-28

Caesarea Philippi, Mk 8:27-33

Following Jesus, Mk 8:31-38

Execution of the Baptist, Mk 6:14-29

The Sower,<the Weeds>, the Seed growing Secretly, Mk 4:1-9, 26-29

Woes over Unrepentant Cities
No Ascension for Capharnaum,
Mt 11:20-24

Ascension of Jesus, Lk 24:50-52;
Acts 1:4-11

[Eschatological Discourse retrojected]

In general outline, this is the Resurrection Narrative given in Luke, but as Lk 24:47 does not represent the opinion of M2 and is clearly an insertion (the disciples are not witnesses of the preaching to all nations), it was probably added by St Luke himself.

In ending his Gospel with the Ascension, M2 may have taken his cue from Peter, who, when calling for the election of an apostle to replace Judas, specified that the man chosen must be "one of those who have accompanied us during all the time that the Lord Jesus went in and out among us, beginning from the baptism of John until the day when he was taken up from us" (Acts 1:22-23). But the evangelists do not regard every single Gospel story, or every single Resurrection appearance, as essential to the apostolic witness. No doubt St Peter wanted the twelfth apostle to be capable of answering any questions that arose about all that happened between the baptism of John and the Ascension. Even the discovery of the Empty Tomb was not regarded as an essential part of the apostolic witness. To judge from the Acts of the Apostles and the Epistles of St Paul, the earliest preaching did not make use of it.

M2, who retrojected the Sermon on the Mount and the Missionary Discourse, including Mt 10:23, was probably also responsible for moving the Eschatological Discourse to its place at the end of the public ministry, just after Jesus had left the temple for the last time. At the time of writing (c. AD 45), the crisis caused by Caligula had passed, but it was likely that another attempt would be made to set up an idolatrous statue of a Roman emperor in the temple. The predictions made in the Discourse had not yet been falsified by history. By retrojecting it and attributing it to Jesus himself, M2 no doubt expected to enhance its persuasiveness.

By ending with the Ascension, M2 left the Baptist's initial prophecy of Spirit-baptism unfulfilled. So it remains in all three canonical Gospels, and in the Fourth Gospel too, unless Jn 20:22 can be regarded as the fulfilment of John's prophecy.

M3's Revision of the Work of M2

After the Council of Jerusalem, at which the Gentile missions of Paul and Barnabas received official approval, M3 saw the need to revise M2 for the benefit chiefly of Gentile Christians, to show them that Jesus, the Risen Lord, approved of missions into Gentile lands and wanted his disciples to extend the preaching of the Gospel to all nations. M3 decided therefore to end his Gospel, not in Jerusalem, but in "Galilee of the Gentiles", on the very mountain where Jesus gave the Sermon on the Mount. It was probably M3 who inserted, after the Last Supper, Jesus' saying, "After my Resurrection I shall go ahead of you (*proaxo humas*) into Galilee" (Mt 26:32; Mk 14:28), to prepare the reader beforehand for a Resurrection Narrative in which Jesus would not appear to his disciples in Jerusalem. The women at the empty tomb are reminded of this by the angel who announces the Resurrection.

> He is risen from the dead, and behold he is going ahead of you into Galilee; there you will see him. Behold I have told you.
> (Mt 28:7)

> He is going ahead of you into Galilee; there you will see him, as he told you. (Mk 16:7)

But there is a serious difficulty here. In Mt 26:32; Mk 14:28, Jesus' promise does not include the words, "there you will see me." Therefore either the angel misquotes Jesus, or these words were originally part of Mt 26:32; Mk 14:28. It makes a difference. The verb *proago* can mean (1) to go before a group leading them (e.g. Mk 10:32), or (2) to go ahead of a group (leaving them to follow later, as in Mk 6:45). Mt 26:32 is therefore ambiguous. It can mean "I will lead you back to Galilee (as I led you here from Galilee)," or "I will go ahead of you (and be there when you arrive)." The shepherd imagery of Mt 26:31 suggests that sense (1) is intended: "I will lead you back to Galilee, as a shepherd leads his flock." But the angel at the tomb clearly takes the word in sense (2). He gently reproaches the women, saying, "He is not here... he is on his way (*proagei*, present tense) back to Galilee – there you will see him, as he told you!" If Jesus' promise did not include the words, "there you will see me", it was reasonable for the disciples to stay in Jerusalem awaiting his arrival to lead them back to Galilee.

To avoid the conclusion that the angel misquotes Jesus, it is better to assume that in M3 Jesus said beforehand, "After my Resurrection I shall go ahead of you into Galilee, and there you will see me."

In Mt 26:32 Jesus does not say why he will appear to the disciples in Galilee – whether to assure them that he is Risen, or to resume his daily contact with them, or to give them further instructions, or to invest them with new powers. (In the three prophecies of the Passion and Resurrection given them during the later stage of the public ministry, Mk 8:31; 9:31; 10:33-34, Jesus does not even say that the disciples will see him again after he has risen from the dead.)

THE EXPECTATIONS OF M3

As a consequence of the Council's decision, then, it was necessary to purge the Gospel of M2's prejudice against the Gentile missions. M3 therefore made changes in various parts of the Gospel.

- He rejected the Infancy Narrative of M2 and introduced a new one, in which wise men from afar welcome the kingdom in the form of a child.

- In the preaching of John the Baptist, he inserted Mt 3:9, which interrupts the imagery of fruit-bearing trees: "Do not say to yourselves, 'We have Abraham for our father,' for I tell you, God could rise up from these stones children to raise Abraham." The universalism of St Paul is here read back into the preaching of the Baptist. (Gal 3:5-29 is Paul's answer to the questions, "Who are the heirs of Abraham?")

- In the Galilean Narrative, M3 introduced the longer version of Jesus' Rejection at Nazareth (Lk 4:16-29), in which Jesus points out that what happened in the time of Elijah and Elisha is happening again. His rejection at Nazareth prefigures his rejection by Israel as a whole – and his acceptance by Gentiles.[25]

- M3 retained the Sermon on the Mount, but in the passage on the Law he inserted an important qualifying clause: "Until heaven and earth pass away, not a jot or tittle shall pass away from the Law, until all is accomplished (*heos an panta genetai*)." And when Jesus had fulfilled all the prophecies by his death, M3 gave words to his last cry: "All is accomplished (*tetelestai*)." The death of Christ was the end of the Law for all who believe (Rom 10:4).

- M3 supplied an "Explanation" of the parable of the Weeds, which conceals its possible application to Paul and his Gentile converts (Mt 13:34-43). It treats every detail of the story as allegorical except the central dialogue in which the lord declares the sower of weeds to be "an enemy." The devil is introduced to bear the blame. The main purpose of the selective decoding of the allegory is to rule out the anti-Pauline interpretation of it.

- He inserted Jesus' Discourse on What defiles a Man (Mt 15:10-19) just before his departure into the Gentile region of Tyre and Sidon, to imply that his disciples are released from the restraints imposed on Jewish missionaries by Jewish food laws.

- In the Eschatological Discourse he inserted the statement that "This Gospel of the kingdom will be proclaimed in the whole world as a witness to all the nations, and then the end will come" (Mt 24:14). He may not, however, have thought that the evangelisation of the whole world would take a long time. St Paul seems to have thought that already in AD 58, when he wrote the Epistle to the Romans, he had completed a large part of the job, "from Jerusalem right round to Illyricum" (Rom 15:19). If it was merely a matter of planting the seed and moving on (Mk 4:26-29), M3 may have thought that the Parousia would occur quite soon after the fall of Jerusalem.

THE RESURRECTION NARRATIVE OF M3:
from the Empty Tomb to the Mountain in Galilee

M3 decided, then, to include no Appearance of Jesus to his disciples in Jerusalem, but to make Jesus send them back to Galilee. An angel appears to Mary Magdalene (with or without other women) at the tomb and makes her the bearer of a message, "the Galilee precept," ordering the disciples to meet Jesus in Galilee on a certain mountain. Accepting her word, they believe in the Resurrection, and believing, they get up and go to Galilee, where they meet Jesus on the mountain (Mt 28:16). From there he sends his disciples to teach all nations what he has taught them, while awaiting his return as Judge in the distant future.

As a result of his omissions, M3 is left with an extremely brief Resurrection Narrative. He suppresses any suggestion that the disciples and the holy women were not expecting the Resurrection, or that the disciples refused to believe the women's report. The reader of this Gospel alone would imagine that the women and the disciples remembered Jesus' repeated prophecies of his Resurrection.

The women go to the tomb, not as in Mk 16:1 to anoint the body of Jesus, but "to view the tomb" (Mt 28:1). They are told that Jesus is risen from the dead, and they carry to his disciples the message, "He is going ahead of you (*proagei*) into Galilee; there you will see him." The disciples, like Joseph in the Infancy Narrative, get up and go at once. In this way M3 avoids the question what Jesus was doing all day between his appearance to the women at dawn and his appearance to the disciples in the late evening. He has no need of the story of Cleopas and his companion and is able to concentrate on Jesus and the Eleven.

M3's decision to omit the appearance of Jesus to his disciples in Jerusalem involved a serious loss. The Appearance of Jesus to the Ten on Easter evening is the occasion when he completes the ordination or creation of a new priesthood. He has previously given them power of binding and loosing (Mt 18:18), that is, of declaring what is sinful and what is not; in the appearance on Easter evening he gives them power of forgiving or refusing forgiveness. These are powers which he exercised himself and now communicates to his disciples, "a new teaching invested with power" (Mk 1:27). Just as the priests of the old covenant were charged to teach the Law and the means of forgiveness provided by the Law, so Jesus' disciples are charged to teach and apply the teachings of Jesus and to exercise the means of forgiveness he has provided. (When M3 wrote, the priestly character of Jesus' disciples, and of the elders and overseers of the churches, had not been recognised.)

At the appointed time and place in Galilee, Jesus appears to the disciples as a figure of great dignity, perhaps transfigured, and they, fearing to approach him, fall down in worship. Whereupon he approaches them and says:

> All power is given to me in heaven and on earth. Going therefore make disciples of all nations, teaching them to observe all I have enjoined on you.
> And behold, I am with you all days to the end of the age.

In this scene, which recalls the third Temptation (Mt 4:8-10), the power of Jesus given him by the Father extends through all space and all time; the rules of conduct he has given are for all nations, in all centuries, everywhere.

In M3 this is the one and only appearance of the Risen Jesus to his disciples, and it does not end with a command to return to Jerusalem. The end and climax of his Gospel is the scene on the mountain in Galilee of the Gentiles. M3 does not wish to represent the Gentile churches as the creations of the Church of Jerusalem. He chooses therefore to end his Gospel with the Appearance in Galilee. This tableau, reflecting the decision of the Council of Jerusalem, as interpreted by Paul (Gal 2:1-9), makes a fine conclusion to a Gospel designed to explain the origin and legitimacy of churches in Gentile lands.

In M3, the Appearance on the Mountain becomes a theological construction embodying the will of Christ as made known by his Holy Spirit at the Council of Jerusalem. It also becomes the end of the Gospel. Each of the evangelists has his own idea about where the Gospel-story should end.

Finally, to explain why the universal commission was not known before the Council of Jerusalem (which would have been superfluous if the commission had been known), M3 may have closed with the sentence, "But they said nothing to anyone, for they were afraid" (Mk 16:8), or perhaps with "But they remained silent and told no one in those days anything of what they had seen" (Lk 9:36). Such was the situation before Pentecost. It was not safe to announce that they represented a kingdom that claimed power over all nations. During this period the disciples experienced remarkable impunity. None of them was arrested or persecuted.

In M3 (and consequently in M4) little remained of M1's parallelism:

Gadarene Exorcism, Mk 5:1-13 Mt 8:28-34	Empty Tomb, Mt 28:1-8
Herdsmen flee to city, Mk 5:14-17 [Cured Man sent home, Mk 5:18-20]	Guards flee to city, Mt 28:11-15
Healing of Paralytic, Mt 9:1-8 Calling of Matthew, Mt 9:9-13 New wine in new skins, Mt 9:27-31	[Appearance to Ten in Jerusalem]

Raising of Jairus's Daughter, Mt 9:18-26	
Cure of Two Blind Men, Mt 9:27-31	[Emmaus]
Healing of a Dumb Man, Mt 9:32-34	
Compassion of Jesus,[26]	Appearance on Mountain,
Mt 9:35-38	Mt 28:16-17
Sending of the Twelve, Mt 10:1-41[26]	Teach all nations, Mt 28:16-20

The prohibition against going to the Gentiles or entering any city of the Samaritans (10:5) is withdrawn by the universal commission in 28:19-20.

M3 saw that the outcome of Jesus' ministry was not, as M1 and M2 expected, a renewed Judaism centred upon Jerusalem,[27] but rather the creation of a world-wide network of communities or "churches," that is, assemblies of people "called out" from the midst of sinful populations to serve God by obeying the words of Jesus. This was the "New Israel" of which the twelve were to be rulers, sitting, metaphorically, on twelve thrones. Each community, and the network as a whole, was to be conspicuous like a city on a hill, an example to all who beheld it.

Reading the story two millennia later, the reader may regret the tone of Pauline triumphalism that had crept into the final scene (cf. Eph 1:10). Although the Gospel has spread far and wide in the West, most of the non-Western civilisations retain their traditional religions or have been won over by Islam, the coming of which the evangelists did not foresee. The frustrated universalist claims of Christianity and of Islam are at the root of the age-old antagonism between Christianity and Islam.[28]

M3's RESURRECTION NARRATIVE AND HIS INFANCY NARRATIVE

M3 contrived to make his Resurrection Narrative match his Infancy Narrative in a reverse parallelism, thus:

A   Annunciation to Joseph, Mt 1:18-25
B   Report of the Magi, Mt 2:1-12
C   Flight into Egypt, Mt 2:13-15
                Slaying of the Innocents, Mt 2:16-18
                Return to Galilee, Mt 2:19-23 &
                Finding in Temple, Lk 2:41-52

C'   Burial of Jesus, Mt 27:56-61
                Guard at Tomb, Mt 7:62-66
                Resurrection and Return to Galilee, Mt 28:1-18
B'   Report of the Guards, Mt 28:11-15
A'   Commissioning of the Disciples, Mt 28:16-20

        (C and C' are "sandwich constructions")

A – A'

Jesus is announced in the earlier text as Emmanuel, God-with-us, and in the later text he promises to be "with" his disciples always. He is announced as the Saviour of his people in A, and in A' he offers baptism and discipleship to people of all nations who become his people through faith and baptism.

B – B'

Wise men from the East, Gentiles, announce in Jerusalem the birth of the Messiah. The chief priests know the prophecy of his birth, but they do not get up and go out to Bethlehem. In the later passage, soldiers, presumably Roman Gentiles, announce the Resurrection of Jesus in Jerusalem, and the chief priests who know of Jesus' prophecy (Mt 27:63), do not go outside the walls to investigate.

C – C'

This pair of texts links the Flight into Egypt with Jesus' withdrawal from Israel into the region of death. In the earlier text Herod makes an attempt to destroy Jesus, but Jesus escapes; then an angel sends Joseph back to Israel, and a second vision tells him to seek safety in Galilee. In the later passage another Joseph and another Mary place the body of Jesus in a tomb. The chief priests make an attempt to keep him there, but Jesus escapes. Then he returns to the land of the living. Through an angelic message he tells his disciples to withdraw to the safety of Galilee. The women here reveal their faith in the same way as Joseph before, by getting up and going.

As was shown in *Gospel Challenges*, pp. 24-26, in M3 the Infancy Narrative included the Loss and Finding in the Temple. What Jesus says to his sorrowing mother when she finds him is exactly what he might have said to the women who visit the tomb: "Why seek me? Did you not know that I must be in my Father's house?" M3 probably shared the view implied in Lk 23:43 that the Spirit of Jesus ascended immediately from the Cross to the presence of the Father.

The Resurrection Narrative of M4 (canonical Matthew):
from the Empty Tomb to the Mountain in Galilee

There are several peculiarities about the canonical text.

- The angel appears in glory (Mt 28:3) but Jesus does not. (The appearance of the angel, as described here, recalls the appearance of Jesus as described in the Transfiguration narrative, Mt 17:2. Taken in reverse order, the two texts together illustrate Mt 22:30, "Risen from the dead, they are like angels in heaven.")

- The angel declares that Jesus is not "here" because he is on his way to Galilee, and will be seen "there." But Jesus immediately falsifies the angel's statement by appearing to Mary Magdalene here at the tomb.

- In 28:10 Jesus says nothing new; he gives Mary Magdalene a modified version of what the angel has already said to her.

- 28:15b looks like a comment written long after the event. A similar phrase is used in Mt 27:8. In these two texts the chief priests use their money to bring about the arrest of Jesus and to hush up reports of his Resurrection.

- It is surprising that the guards report first to the chief priests. If they are Roman soldiers, they should report to a Roman officer. This narrative (28:11-14), inherited from M1, is best regarded as a slightly inept fiction designed to explain the origin of the common Jewish response to the Christian explanation of the Empty Tomb. The idea of soldiers bearing witness to what happened while they were asleep on guard duty struck St Augustine as positively laughable.

- The guards are said to have reported to the chief priests "all that had happened," but they were not in a position to do so.

The first three of these peculiarities are probably the results of one and the same cause: M4, having learned from elsewhere that Jesus appeared first to Mary Magdalene, inserted Mt 28:9-10, out of respect for this tradition. In his insertion, he omitted to give any description of Jesus' dress or appearance, and not knowing what Jesus said to Mary, simply made him repeat the Galilee precept. He probably meant the angel's message to be understood in the sense that "Jesus is about to set off for Galilee." The present tense can easily extend to the immediate future, and he may have felt that there was nothing unusual in Jesus' appearing unexpectedly – as he will at his Second Coming (Mt 24:44). (In M1, the disciples went to Galilee expecting to see Jesus on a certain day on a certain mountain, but he surprised seven of them by appearing before dawn on the sea shore.)

In the Report of the Guards, M4 may be responsible for the insertion of the "all" in 28:11.

The guards had not witnessed "all that had happened." All they could report was that there was an earthquake and that a terrifying angel came down and rolled away the stone; they themselves were stunned and "became like dead men." They did not hear the announcement of the Resurrection or the Galilee precept. When they regained their senses, the tomb was empty. From these limited data the chief priests inferred that the body had been stolen. The guards were bribed to hush up the story of the angel and the earthquake.

From the narrative of the Appearance on the Mountain, M4 removed the Transfiguration of Jesus and placed it shortly after Peter's Confession at Caesarea Philippi, to show that the Father revealed his Son to Peter long before he did the same for Paul. The vocabulary of Mt 16:16-17 bears a marked resemblance to that of Gal 1:15-16.

To the universal commission to teach all nations M4 added the command to baptise them using the Trinitarian formula. This was not in use till some decades after Pentecost.

If M3 ended with "But they said nothing to anyone, for they were afraid," M4 deleted it. He is kind to the male disciples. In his Resurrection Narrative they do not disbelieve what they are told, and they are not reproached for unbelief.

The Resurrection Narrative of Mark:
the Empty Tomb, and the Longer Ending

The original text of Mark ends abruptly at 16:8 with the statement that the women who visited the tomb "told no one anything, for they were afraid." Probably the last page of the archetypal manuscripts was lost before copies were made, and the so-called "Longer Ending" (16:9-19) was added by a later writer. He makes a fresh beginning and introduces Mary Magdalene as if she were a new character.

> Rising up early on the first day of the week, he appeared first to Mary Magdalene, from whom he had expelled seven demons.

This detail may not, however, be totally irrelevant, if the writer was summarising a text that matched the Gadarene Exorcism with this first Appearance. At the end of the Gadarene story, the man from whom Jesus has expelled a legion of devils wishes to remain with Jesus but is sent away with a message for his own people, just as Mary Magdalene, who would like to remain, is sent away with a message for the disciples. Next the writer briefly mentions the two travellers returning from Emmaus and says that the disciples did not believe their report either. Evidently this later writer is not summarising Matthew or Luke. He may have known from memory what the original ending contained.

The truncated Narrative in Mk 16:1-8 divides into two parts. The first is about what the women expected to find and what they found – not the mangled body of Jesus, but a radiant young man dressed in white. The second is about what the young man said. He told the women to calm down and mildly reproached them for seeking Jesus there, reminding them that Jesus had said that after rising from the dead he would go ahead of them to Galilee, and they would see him there (not here). But the women's emotions were not calmed; they fled from the tomb "and told no one anything, for they were afraid." If this puzzling sentence belongs here, it must be intended to explain why the Resurrection did not immediately come to public knowledge; the only story circulated in Jerusalem at the time was the one put out by the chief priests.

The original ending may have continued: "But Mary (Magdalene) stood outside weeping" (cf. Jn 20:11);[29] there Jesus appeared to her and repeated the message to be carried to his disciples that they should meet him in Galilee. She reported to the disciples, but they did not believe her. Meanwhile Jesus walks to Emmaus with Cleopas and his companion; he reveals himself to them, and they return to the other disciples but are not believed. Then the story continued as in Mk 16:14-19:

> Later he appeared to the eleven at table and reproached them for their unbelief and hardness of heart in that they had not believed those who had seen him risen.

To judge from the Galilean anticipation (Mk 4:35-41), this rebuke was a part of the earliest written tradition. It is consistent with the disciples' incomprehension throughout the public ministry in Mark. In the continuation, Jesus gives the disciples their universal commission:

> And he said to them, "Going into the whole world, proclaim the gospel to the whole creation. He who believes and is baptised will be saved; he who does not believe will be condemned."

The call to believe and be baptised is the necessary practical conclusion to the whole Gospel, as in Acts 2:37-38 and Jn 20:31.

The writer of the Longer Ending, and probably Mark too, still expected the preaching of the Gospel to be confirmed by miracles, since the text concludes:

> "These signs will accompany believers: in my name they will cast out devils, speak in new tongues, pick up snakes, and if they drink poison it will not harm them; they will lay hands on the sick, and they will be well." The Lord Jesus, after speaking to them, was taken up into heaven and sat at the right hand of God, but they went forth and preached everywhere, the Lord cooperating and confirming the word by the signs that accompanied them.

The writer seems to know the story of Paul's adventure with the viper on the island of Malta in AD 62 (Acts 28:3-6).

The Resurrection Narrative of Luke:
from the Empty Tomb to the Ascension

The Resurrection Narrative of St Luke's Gospel consists of:

Lk 24-1-11   The Women at the Empty Tomb; they report to the disciples.
Lk 24:12*   Peter visits the tomb and wonders.
Lk 24:13-35 The Journey to Emmaus and Return.
Lk 24:36-49 Jesus appears to the disciples in the evening; sends them to all nations; tells them to await the coming of the Spirit.
Lk 24:50-53 The Ascension of Jesus into heaven.

*24:12 is missing in many manuscripts and may not be authentic.

As was mentioned above, St Luke chose to follow the Resurrection Narrative of M2, with one important addition (24:47). He does not here follow Mark even as far as Mk 16:8. In preparation for the scene at the Empty Tomb, he omits Mk 14:28, where Jesus promises that after his Resurrection he will go ahead of his disciples to Galilee. The two angels that appear at the tomb refer back, not to what Jesus said in Mk 14:28, but to his three earlier prophecies of his crucifixion and Resurrection; the wording used in Mk 8:31, 9:31, and 10:33-34 reappears in Lk 24:7. At the angels' prompting, the women remember the prophecies and return to report to the apostles what has happened. The apostles treat their words as "nonsense" (*hosei leros*). But this need not mean that they treated the women with contempt. In Acts 12:15, when Peter, just escaped from prison, appears at the house of John Mark's mother, and the maid named Rose goes indoors to say that Peter is outside, she is told "You are mad!" Both expressions simply mean that the hearers are staggered and what is reported is, as we say, "unbelievable".

Luke 21:12 may not be authentic, but it fits remarkably well. It reads like a summary of Jn 20:3-10, a story that may well have been known to St Luke. "But Peter rising up ran to the tomb, and bending down saw the linen cloths apart, and went away wondering over what had happened." "Wondering" describes a state half-way to belief. Probably at this point Jesus appeared to him, but St Luke has unaccountably omitted the story, apart from the brief reference to it in Lk 24:34. An anomalous result of this omission is that the first male witness of the Resurrection in Luke is Cleopas, not one of the Twelve. He sees the Risen Jesus twice, first at Emmaus, and again in the upper room in Jerusalem.[30]

The diffuse narrative of the Journey to Emmaus is disproportionately long and disappointingly uninformative. Out of the fifty-three verses in Lk 24, twenty-three are devoted to Jesus' appearance to two disciples who were not apostles or official witnesses of the Resurrection, while the appearance to Peter is mentioned but not described. Much of the story is repetition of what has happened up to this point. Then there is a discussion of Scripture texts that foretell the Passion and Resurrection, but the texts are not quoted. Jesus is finally recognised in the breaking of bread; but at once he vanishes, before the two disciples have any opportunity to ask any question about what Jesus has experienced between his death and reappearance. In its general structure, this narrative resembles Acts 8:26-40, Philip's encounter with the Ethiopian Eunuch. The one incident is the prototype of the Eucharistic liturgy, the other of the Baptismal liturgy.

One part of the Emmaus story, however, contains an important comment on all the Resurrection Appearances. In Lk 24:44-47 Jesus chides the two travellers as "foolish and slow of heart"; they should have been expecting him to rise on the third day, and on the third day itself they should have believed that he was risen, even before they heard the angel's message. The implication of this passage is that on the three or more occasions when Jesus predicted his passion and death, he at the same time explained that this was what the prophets had foretold.[31] Even the sending of the angel messenger was a concession to their weakness; his announcement ought to have moved them to recall what Jesus had predicted.

When Jesus appears to the disciples in Jerusalem, his first aim is to convince them that they are not seeing a ghost but a real body: he invites them to feel his flesh and bones, and he eats a piece of fish in their presence. Then again, as on the road to Emmaus, he explains that his death and Resurrection are the fulfilment of the Law and the Prophets. At the very least, the evangelist wishes to assure Jewish readers that they will not be abandoning Judaism if they become Christians; Christianity is in fact the true Judaism (cf. Rom 2:28-29). But indirectly, the evangelist may be suggesting to his readers that if the narrative of Jesus' ministry and death has persuaded them to believe in Jesus, they really have no need of any description of his Resurrection Appearances.

At the end of the scene, St Luke inserts the command to offer repentance and forgiveness of sins to all nations (baptism is not mentioned). The introduction of the universal commission (24:47) is the chief divergence of St Luke from the Resurrection Narrative of M2. Jesus announces the evangelisation of the Gentiles in an oblique way as prophesied and thereby enjoined by the Scriptures.

> He said to them: "These are my words that I spoke to you while still with you, that all that is written in the Law of Moses and the prophets and psalms must be fulfilled. Then he opened their mind to understand the Scriptures. And he said to them: "Thus it is written that the Christ must suffer and rise from the dead on the third day <and repentance for the forgiveness of sins must be proclaimed in his name to all the nations. Beginning from Jerusalem,> you are witnesses of these things. And behold I am sending the promise of the Father upon you. But you must remain in the city until you are clothed with power from on high.[32]

Strictly speaking, the eleven cannot be witnesses of the evangelisation of all nations (which the inserted verse might suggest); they are the witnesses of the Death and Resurrection of Jesus, and they must begin their proclamation of his death and Resurrection from Jerusalem, no doubt because Isaiah (2:3) prophesied that "Out of Zion shall go forth the Law, and the Word of the Lord from Jerusalem." St Luke rejected M3's Galilean ending to the Gospel out of respect for this prophecy and because he knew that in fact the apostolic witness to the fulfilment of the Scriptures was first given in Jerusalem, not in Capharnaum or any other city of Galilee.

St Luke also saw that at the time of the Ascension the promise of John the Baptist remained unfulfilled; therefore neither the Appearance on the mountain in Galilee, nor the Ascension was a fully satisfactory ending to the Gospel-story. A continuation was required.

The Resurrection Narrative of the Acts of the Apostles:
from the Resurrection to Pentecost

The Forty Days, Acts 1:1-3

The Author of the book that was St Luke's main source for the Acts of the Apostles 1:1-23:11[33] presupposes knowledge of a Gospel in which after his Resurrection Jesus appeared to his disciples several times over a period of forty days, i.e. he assumes that his reader has read something like the Resurrection Narrative of M1 reconstructed above. During these forty days Jesus explained the Scriptures (as in Lk 24:27, 44-45) and gave instructions to the disciples. It appears from the sequel in Acts that he did not tell them that when on missionary journeys they were free to enter Gentile houses and eat with Gentiles, nor did he give any ruling on the question whether Gentile converts should be circumcised and required to obey the Law of Moses. Nor is there any indication that he told Peter to appoint a successor to Judas or to institute the sharing of property.

The Final Supper, Acts 1:4

The meaning of 1:4 is uncertain. "While staying (or eating) with them…" (RSV) "While he was in their company…" (NEB, for *sunaulizomenos*?) But the doubtful verb (*sunalizomenos*) may mean "While taking salt with them…," i.e. while sharing a meal with them" (cf. Acts 10:41).

Renewal of the Baptist's Promise, Acts 1:4-5

Jesus says to his assembled disciples, "Wait here (in Jerusalem) for the fulfilment of the Father's promise which you heard from me: 'John's baptism was with water, but you will be baptised with the Holy Spirit within these not many days.'" Since Jesus does not renew John's promise in any of the four Gospels, the reference must be to an instruction given earlier in the forty days, or in a lost Gospel.

The Disciples' Question and Jesus' Answer, Acts 1:6-7

The assembled disciples ask Jesus, "Lord will you at this time restore the kingdom of Israel?" The question appears to arise out of Jesus' promise that they would receive Spirit-baptism within a few days. If they took the promised event to be the fulfilment of the prophecy of John the Baptist, they might well expect it to be the Day when the wicked would be destroyed and the repentant rescued into the kingdom of God (Mt 3:11-12).

Yet Acts 1:6 is puzzling. It is hardly credible that at this late date the disciples can still imagine that Jesus is about to re-establish the Davidic monarchy in Jerusalem. Probably their question means: Will the outpouring of the Spirit be the inauguration of the new Davidic kingdom in Israel? In a sense it will, but Jesus does not give a direct answer, no doubt because they have in their minds a mistaken picture of what the new kingdom will be like.

The Universal Commission, Acts 1:8

This sentence, which can hardly be construed as a continuation of the thought of 1:7, may be an insertion by St Luke to give readers of his Acts an indication of what they can expect in the following pages: the Gospel will be carried from Jerusalem through Judea and Samaria "to the ends of the earth." In fact, it is carried only as far as Rome, but St Luke probably knew that Paul's ambition was to go on to Spain (Rom 15:26). The insertion is, however, misleading, in that the disciples do not, in the following pages, act as if they had been instructed to spread out through the world bearing witness to Jesus. Peter, James and John remain in Jerusalem. The "deacons" remain there until Paul's persecution drives them out. It is they and Paul who fulfil the charge given in 1:8. Even in neighbouring Samaria the work of evangelisation is begun by Philip, not by any of the twelve. In the first seven chapters of Acts, the apostles act as if still bound by Jesus' prohibition in Mt 10:5, "Do not go the way to the Gentiles, and do not enter any city of the Samaritans."

The Acts of the Apostles is not, as its title suggests, the story of how the eleven apostles, commanded by the risen Lord to go forth and teach all nations, promptly and obediently went forth and did so. The reader finds, instead, that for some years they regard the Church as a movement within Judaism, with one or two privileged Gentiles like the centurion Cornelius admitted to baptism, just as in the ministry of Jesus miracles were granted by way of exception to the centurion at Capharnaum and to the Syro-Phoenician Woman. The writing of Gospels began in this very early period. The Acts of the Apostles is really the story of how this small group within Judaism gradually learned, through the guidance of the Spirit, and to its own surprise, that it was destined to expand into Samaria, Syria (Antioch), Asia, Greece and Italy. Once started, the expansion goes steadily ahead with only two major setbacks, namely the controversy over circumcision and the Law, and Paul's failure to found a church at Athens.

The Ascension, Acts 1:9

Though the disciples do not recognise it, and perhaps St Luke himself did not recognise it,[34] the Author from whom St Luke is borrowing recognises that Jesus ascending into heaven is the eternal High Priest entering the heavenly Holy of Holies to make intercession for sinners baptised in his name (Heb 4:14-5:6). The Author insinuates this by matching 1:1-11 with 22:17-23:11, where Paul fails to recognise the Jewish High Priest (23:3). The seemingly pointless dialogue in 22:28 is probably allegorical. Paul escaping torture thanks to his Roman citizenship represents the Christian who escapes the penalties of his sins thanks to his heavenly citizenship (Phil 3:20), bought for him at a great price (1 Cor 6:20; 7:23) by one who was a citizen of heaven by birthright. Jesus ascends into heaven by birthright and by merit, the beloved Son, in whom his Father is well pleased.

At the end of the later text, Jesus appears to Paul by night and says: "Take heart. As you have testified about me in Jerusalem, so you must bear witness also at Rome." This was the end of St Luke's main source, written about AD 58.

The Angel's Message, Acts 1:9-10

The angel tells the men (*andres*) of Galilee that Jesus will come in the same way as they saw him go. (It seems they alone were present.) Since Jesus himself predicted that he would return "with the clouds of heaven" (Mk 14:62), it is at least possible that Jesus was transfigured as he ascended.

The First Community, Acts 1:12-14

The author assumes that the reader knows, perhaps from an earlier Gospel,[35] how the family of Jesus was won over to believe in him. It is not explained how this little community grew to one hundred and twenty (1:15).

The End of Judas, Acts 1:16-20

A different version of this story is told in Mt 27: 3-10. There the chief priests buy the Potter's Field; here Judas himself. Matthew emphasises the callousness of the chief priests.

The Choice of Matthias, Acts 1:21-26

The choice of Matthias has no consequences later in the book. Its main purpose seems to be to explain why Paul was never acknowledged to be the twelfth Apostle. The Author of Acts 1:1-32:11

may have thought that Peter acted precipitately in choosing a twelfth apostle before receiving the Holy Spirit. In 22:17-23:11, at the right time, Jesus himself commissions Paul to preach to the Gentiles.

The Coming of the Spirit at Pentecost, Acts 2:1-13

What happens here is not at all what John the Baptist expected. He predicted a terrifying deluge of wind and fire (*pneumati kai puri*) that would destroy the wicked but leave the repentant unharmed for admission to the kingdom of God (Mt 3:11-12). What happens here makes the unrepentant laugh and jeer at the believers: "These men are full of new wine!" Nevertheless, the Pentecost story is linked to John's prophecy by Jesus' saying in 1:5. One must conclude, therefore, that John's prophecy is fulfilled, but in a sense quite other than what he intended.

In 2:5 the Author probably wrote "Living in Jerusalem were devout men from every nation under heaven," and Luke inserted "Jews" before "devout men." The Author did not mean his list to be a list of Jewish pilgrims from all the nations in question. Only towards the end of his list does he include "Jews and proselytes." The Author intended to show that in the earliest days after Pentecost, the Gospel was preached to all nations, especially by Peter. In Acts 15:7 Peter may well be referring back to these "very early days."

Peter's Speech at Pentecost, Acts 2:14-42

It is remarkable that Peter does not explain the phenomena of Pentecost as the fulfilment of John the Baptist's prophecy, and that neither in this speech nor in his next does he mention Jesus' post-Resurrection Appearances to his disciples. It seems that they were not part of the very earliest Christian apologetic. But that soon changed; see 1 Cor 15: 3-8.

In 2:24 Peter makes an emphatic announcement, which translations often consign to an undertone, because syntactically it is a subordinate clause. Rhetorically, however, it can be a climax:[36]

> Jesus of Nazareth, a man whose mission to you was attested by God through the miracles, wonders and signs that God did by his hands among you, as you yourselves know –
>
> This Jesus, with God's previous knowledge and permission,
>
> YOU delivered into the hands of lawless men to be crucified and killed –
>
> *HIM God has raised up, loosing the bonds of death!*
>
> Exalted at God's right hand, he has received from the Father the promised gift of the Holy Spirit, and has poured it out as you see and hear.

This was the first public announcement of the Resurrection in Jerusalem. This is what cut the hearers to the heart. It has been suggested that the rejection of Jesus by the people of Jerusalem, who had been admirers and defenders of Jesus during his days in the temple, was a temporary lapse, like that of Peter. When Peter reproached them with it, they were stung with remorse, as Peter was earlier.[37]

Peter's speech rounding off the Gospel-story ends, like the Baptist's preaching at the beginning, with penitents asking, "What then shall we do?" (Lk 3:10; Acts 2:37). The Baptist replied by urging the sharing of property: "Let him that has two cloaks share with him who has none, and him who has food likewise." Peter's first response is, "Repent and be baptised." But soon after that comes the sharing of property. The common life of the early community as described in 2:42-47 and 4:32-37 is Peter's effort to fulfil the ideal set before the disciples by Jesus in Mt 5:14, "You are the light of the world. A city built on a hilltop cannot remain hid… So let your light shine before men that they see your good works and give glory to your Father in heaven" – words not included in Luke's Gospel.

Afterword

This investigation of the Resurrection Narratives shows that the stories presented in Matthew, Luke and John are not imaginary tales that conflict with one another and undermine the credibility of the evangelists. Each of the evangelists has made a selection from a larger collection of traditional stories that go back to eye-witnesses, and has adapted his own selection to support his view of the Church. M1 and still more M2 presented a conservative view of the Church, which was acceptable to many Jewish Christians or Christian Jews down to the time of the Council of Jerusalem. M3 and the canonical evangelists all accept the Council's decision and modify the Resurrection Narrative to show that the commission to teach all nations is the will of the risen Lord, not revealed while he was "still with" his disciples. During his ministry on earth his own commission was to the lost sheep of the house of Israel (Mt 15:24); after his Resurrection his power was extended to all nations, and he himself cancelled the previous restrictions he had placed on the commission he gave to his disciples. The scenes in which he does so are modifications of traditional scenes, made in the light of the Church's experience and under the guidance of the Holy Spirit.

In some ways the Resurrection Narratives are surprising, perhaps disappointing. Jesus holds himself aloof from his disciples, friends and family.

He quickly dispatches Mary Magdalene with a message. In none of the Appearances does he permit any familiarity. On the road to Emmaus he calls the two travellers "foolish and slow of heart"; at table in Emmaus he vanishes as soon as he is recognised. What happened during his first appearance to penitent Peter is not recorded. In Jerusalem he reproaches his disciples for unbelief. At the sea of Tiberias, reverence inhibits them from asking, "Who are you?" and when Peter asks a question, Jesus rebuffs him with "What is that to you?" He does not seek reunion with his own family. In the Transfiguration, he converses with Moses and Elijah, not with his disciples; as they hesitate to approach him, he condescends to approach them. When he descends from the mountain, he is impatient with his other disciples and exclaims, "How long shall I be with you, how long endure you?" He has become Christos Pantocrator.

NOTES

1 The Two-Source Theory postulates a second source (Q), from which come the stories and sayings common to Matthew and Luke but absent from Mark. However, there are no "Q-materials" in the Resurrection Narratives.
2 There is also a structural link between Jn 20:28-31 and 10:29-39. In 10:38 Jesus urges his hearers to believe in him on the strength of his works, as the evangelist does in 20:30-31.
3 There is no explicit mention of Baptism in this Resurrection Narrative.
4 See Georg Bertram, "Die Himmelfahrt Jesu vom Kreuz aus," in Festschrift A Deissmann, p. 191.
5 The names of James and John may have been introduced when the story was retrojected into the later Galilean ministry.
6 Cf. R.G. Hamerton-Kelly, *Pre-Existence, Wisdom, and the Son of Man* (1973), p. 49.
7 Albert Schweitzer, *The Quest of the Historical Jesus* (rpt. 1963), p. ix. Shocked by this discovery, he concluded that Jesus was not omniscient, whereupon he abandoned traditional Christianity and went off to Africa to care for the sick. Many would-be propagandists of today find themselves in a similar predicament: no longer sure that Jesus was the eternal Son of God made man, or that he rose from the dead and reigns at God's right hand, or that he will one day return to earth, or that his death was vicarious satisfaction for the sins of humankind. What they do wish to propagate is the Christian ethic of sharing wealth, renouncing revenge and violence, honest speech, fidelity in marriage, respect for children, and care for the poor, the sick, and the aged.
8 Responsibility for the death of the Baptist is here placed on all the Jews, as is responsibility for the death of Jesus in Mt 27:25.
9 R. Bultmann, *History of the Synoptic Tradition*, p. 157.
10 Gaius ordered Petronius, Governor of Syria, to set up in the temple at Jerusalem a statue of Zeus with the features of Gaius. For details, see *Gospel Challenges*, pp. 221-27.
11 The author of the Emmaus narrative, however, appears to have thought that Resurrection Appearances ought not to have been necessary to convince the disciples that he was risen; they should have known that the predictions of the prophets, explained to them by Jesus during his ministry, would certainly be fulfilled. See Lk 24:44-47.
12 The parallel in Mt 2:22 suggests that they are sent to Galilee for their safety.
13 As was shown in *Gospel Challenges*, pp. 85-86, the original Sermon

on the Plain included Lk 11:31-36 and 12:13-34. St Luke removed these passages to fill out one of his reverse parallelisms.

14 Horace, Epistles, I,v,13. See Norman De Witt, *Epicurus and his Philosophy*, 1967, p. 336.

15 Gerard Rochais, *Les recits de Resurrection des morts dans le Nouveau Testament* (Cambridge: Cambridge University Press, 1981), pp. 72-73, conjectures that "already before Mark tradition had understood this miracle in connection with the Resurrection of Jesus." Jesus asks the mourners, "Why are you weeping?" just as in Jn 20:15 he will ask Mary Magdalene after his Resurrection, "Why are you weeping? (Jn 20:15). "These same words pronounced after the Resurrection of Jesus and before the Resurrection of Jairus's daughter indicate that in reality the two miracles are linked, that faith in the Risen Jesus is the guarantee of the Resurrection of the infant."

16 See James R. Edwards, *Markan Sandwiches: The Significance of Interpolations in Markan Narratives*, Novum Testamentum, 31 (1989), pp. 193-216.

17 The Stilling of the Tempest, especially in the Markan version (Mk 4:35-41), points forward to a scene in which Jesus rebukes his disciples for being so cowardly and unbelieving (Mk 16:14).

18 In this reconstructed Resurrection Narrative, as in canonical Matthew, the Transfiguration Narrative follows the ambiguous Mt 16:28, by which either Jesus prophesied that the Son of Man would come as Judge before the death of the last apostle, or predicted the Transfiguration, which took place six days later.

19 The threefold Temptation Narrative was introduced by M2 to show Jesus using the Law to repel each temptation.

20 In Acts 10:38 Peter regards the miracles of Jesus as works of the Spirit.

21 The writer was clearly a law-observing Jew writing for Jewish Christians, since he urges his readers to pray that their flight may not be on a sabbath (Mt 24:20).

22 This Warning also matches Lk 23:28-31 in the Passion Narrative. Both passages are warnings of worse to come if the Jews do not repent.

23 The phrase is strange, since the requirement of circumcision belongs to the covenant granted to Abraham (Gen 17:10-14); it is not mentioned in the Law of Moses.

24 Inserted by M2 to show that even when performing a miracle Jesus required every jot and tittle of the Law to be observed.

25 Jesus' observation that a prophet is not without honour except in his own country holds true of gods as well. The greatest gods of Greece, Zeus, Apollo and Dionysus, all came in from far countries. In ancient times, the remoter parts of the world were totally

mysterious. Cults brought from afar by enthusiastic worshippers gained easy acceptance from worshippers disappointed with their own gods. As Tacitus said, *Omne ignotum pro magnifico.*

26 It is surprising that M3 allowed Mt 10:23 to stand. He may have done so because he saw that by his time the disciples had not made great progress in converting Galilee and Judea. "All Israel" still remained unconverted (Rom 11:26).

27 In St Paul's view, Jerusalem remains "a slave and the mother of slaves" (Gal 4:25-26). The citizenship (*politeuma*) of believers is in heaven (Phil 3:20).

28 See Samuel P. Huntington, *The Clash of Civilizations and the Remaking of World Order* (1996, rpt. 2003), pp. 209-18. When readers immerse themselves in the Gospel story, the intervening millennia fall away, and it seems a splendid thing for the eleven Galileans to set out to conquer the world for Christ. But returning to his own world, he or she is liable to be less sure about attempts to penetrate and transform or even suppress other cultures inspired by other religions and other philosophies.

29 In the Fourth Gospel this transition is awkward (see Jn 20:10-11). Peter and John, who now believe, go off leaving Mary Magdalene still weeping. Why do they not stay to persuade her that Jesus is Risen?

30 According to Eusebius, *Ecclesiastical History,* Bk 3, 11, Cleopas was the brother of Joseph the husband of Mary, and was the father of Simeon, who became leader of the post-70 Christian community of Jerusalem. The Emmaus story may come from the brethren of Jesus.

31 In Mk 9:31, the English translation, "He began to teach them that the Son of Man must suffer many things," conceals the force and position of the Greek *dei:* "He began to teach them: 'It is necessary that the Son of Man shall suffer many things,'" meaning: "It is the will of God declared in Scripture that He shall suffer many things."

32 No doubt Jesus here spoke of the fulfilment of the prophecy of Joel 2:28-32, which Peter has ready and promptly quotes on the morning of Pentecost (Acts 2:17-21).

33 See the Appendix to *Gospel Challenges,* pp. 288-96, on the structure of the two main sections of the Acts of the Apostles.

34 W. Manson, *Jesus the Messiah* (1947), p. 14, observed that "the early Church remembered better than it understood."

35 See *Gospel Challenges,* pp. 138-41, on the implications of Jn 2:12.

36 Suitably read, this sounds like Demosthenes fulminating at the Athenians in his first Olynthiac Oration.

37 R.G. Ascough, *Rejection and Repentance: Peter and the People in Luke's Passion Narrative,* Biblica 74 (1993), pp. 349-68.